SHORTCUTS TO SUCCESS

HISTORY EXAM GUIDE

Leaving Certificate

The Research Study, Document Questions and
Sample Essays

Dermot Lucey

Gill & Macmillan

The Leaving Cert History Examination

As a Leaving Cert History student, you will have to undertake:

* A Research Study Report – 20 per cent of the marks.
* The Leaving Cert History examination paper – 80 per cent of the marks.

The Research Study Report is written into a booklet provided by the State Examinations Commission. Section 1 – Guidelines for Answering the Research Study will guide you through the stages in writing up your Research Study.

The Leaving Cert examination paper has two main parts:

* The documents-based Case Studies.
* Three essays to be answered from Topics chosen by you (or your teacher).

Section 2 – Documents-based Case Studies will help you improve your answers for the documents questions. This section has sample questions and answers. Note: You are studying documents-based case studies from *either* **The USA and the World, 1945–89** *or* **Politics and Society in Northern Ireland, 1949–93**, depending on which year you are sitting your Leaving Cert examination.

Section 3 – Answering Questions on the Topics will help you with guidelines for essay writing and some of the sample answers and essay plans for a variety of topics.

Note: You have to answer one question from each of three Topics.

Contents

Section 1 – Guidelines for Answering the Research Study

Choosing Your Research Study   1

The Outline Plan   3

Evaluation of Sources   10

The Extended Essay   17

Example of an Extended Essay   21

Marking Scheme: Research Study (Higher Level)   26

Section 2 – Document-based Case Studies

Guidelines for Answering Document-based Questions   29

The USA and the World, 1945–89: A Framework for the Case Studies   32

Leaving Cert Examination 2008 and 2009

Case Study: The Montgomery Bus Boycott, 1955–56   35

Case Study: Lyndon Johnson and Vietnam, 1963–68   46

Case Study: The Moon Landing, 1969   56

Sample Answers on the Case Studies: The USA and the World, 1945–89   64

Politics and Society in Northern Ireland, 1949–93: A Framework for the Case
   Studies   74

Leaving Cert Examination 2010 and 2011

Case Study: The Coleraine University Controversy   77

Case Study: The Apprentice Boys of Derry   84

Case Study: The Sunningdale Agreement and the Power-sharing Executive   90

Sample Answers on the Case Studies: Politics and Society in
   Northern Ireland, 1949–93   100

Section 3 – Answering Questions on the Topics

Answering Ordinary Level Questions   114

Answering Higher Level Questions   119

Sample Higher Level Essay and Sample Plans   137

Modern Irish History   137

- Movements for Political and Social Reform, 1870–1914   137

- The Pursuit of Sovereignty and the Impact of Partition, 1912–49   145

- Government, Economy and Society in the Republic of Ireland, 1949–89   148

Modern Europe and the Wider World   152

- Nation States and International Tensions, 1871–1920   152

- Dictatorship and Democracy in Europe, 1920–45   153

- Division and Realignment in Europe, 1945–92   166

- The USA and the World, 1945–89   171

Section 1

GUIDELINES FOR ANSWERING THE RESEARCH STUDY

Your Research Study Report (RSR) can be done on any topic in any period in history. This means you do not have to confine your study to the Topics you are studying for the rest of your exam. For example, you can choose Research Studies from ancient Ireland or Greece, from Chinese or Japanese history, just as you can from modern Irish or European and US history.

In choosing a topic for study, **it is usually better to keep away from Case Studies and Key Personalities**. Why? It is possible that you might lose marks under the heading 'Research Skills: Appropriate depth of investigation'.

However, if you insist on doing a Research Study on a Key Personality, then you should **choose a special aspect of that personality**. For example, instead of doing a RSR on Martin Luther King (a Key Personality in The United States and the Wider World, 1945–89), you could narrow your research study to 'Martin Luther King and the FBI'.

Choose a topic with a **narrow focus** for your Research Study. For example, instead of doing a research study on the War of Independence, 1919–21, it would be better to do the study on the War of Independence in a local area, such as Dublin or Cork.

But very often **the sources will decide what Research Study you will do** – it is difficult to do what you think is an interesting project with poor sources.

WHAT IS A SOURCE?

Everything that survives from the past is a source in history. But for the purposes of the Research Study, you will depend mostly on books, articles and internet sites.

WHERE TO GET SOURCES

The school library, the local library branch (city or county), the main library headquarters, university libraries (if you can get access), books from www.amazon.co.uk and the internet, home, interviews and your teacher are all possible places to get sources.

In general, it is easier to get your information from a short article than from a book.

- There is too much information in a book and it is difficult to condense. It is better to use the article and get some back-up information from a book.
- **Keep a list of sources**.
- Photocopy the cover and title pages of the book or magazine.

BE ORGANISED

Keep a **file or folder** to store:
- Copies of your sources.
- Notes taken from sources.
- Drafts of your essay.

TAKING NOTES

- Concentrate on one or two main sources.
- Write the details of the book/article – author, title, etc. – on top of an A4 page.
- Read the sections of the book/article relevant to your Research Study – use the contents, chapter headings and index to find the information.
- Take brief notes – there is no need to write out full sentences.
- Break the notes down into headings, subheadings and points.
- Underline key words in the notes.
- Combine different sets of notes into one, if necessary.
- Use the notes to plan the structure of your research essay – one main point for each paragraph (see Essay Writing in the Research Study and the Topics, especially pp. 122–28).

WRITING YOUR RESEARCH STUDY

We will go through the writing of the Research Study step by step, using a Research Study on 'The Assassination of President John F. Kennedy, 1963' as an example.

You will eventually write up your completed RSR in a special booklet provided by the State Examinations Commission (SEC) that will be given to you by your teacher. The project must be written up by the end of April of your Leaving Cert exam year (usually the last Friday of April).

- You should get your Research Study done well before this, as you need the weeks up to the final exam in June for revising the topics which will be examined there.

You should **practise writing your project** into a **sample booklet** which your teacher will give you or which you can download from the State Examinations Commission website, www.examinations.ie (it is called the History Coursework Journal).

Doing a draft

- Even though the Outline Plan and the Evaluation of Sources are supposed to be done before writing the essay, this is often not practical.
- Do a draft of the Outline Plan at the beginning, but finish it off properly after you have completed your research essay.

Title

Begin with a **working title**. When you have finished your essay:

- **Make the title suit the content of your essay.**
- **Keep the title** if you are satisfied that the content of your essay matches the title.
- **Change the title** if you have included extra information which does not fit the exact title you began with.
- Include a date(s) where possible, but make sure the date(s) suits the content of the essay.

TEIDEAL AN STAIDÉIR
TITLE OF THE STUDY

Scríobh síos anseo teideal iomlán do Staidéir Thaighde agus na dataí a bhaineann leis, más cuí. Write below the full title, and date parameters where appropriate, of your Research Study.

The Assassination of President John F. Kennedy, 1963

The Outline Plan (15 marks)

The Outline Plan is broken into the following parts:

1. Defines and justifies the proposed subject ⎫
2. Identifies the aims ⎬ 9 marks
3. Indicates the intended approach ⎭
4. Cites the sources to be consulted   6 marks

    Total   =   15 marks

WHAT DO THESE MEAN?

1. (a) **Define:** Says what your project is about.
    (b) **Justify:** Says why it is a worthwhile study.

Example

> *Define and Justify: I intend to research the assassination of President John F. Kennedy (JFK) and the conspiracies which surrounded it since 1963. On 22 November 1963, JFK was fatally wounded in Dallas, Texas. The murder caused national uproar and since then Kennedy has become an icon of the 1960s. This topic is particularly significant because of the manner in which the most powerful political leader in a democratic country such as the US was killed, the controversy it provoked and the impact of Kennedy's death on the US.*

2. Aims: Here you lay out the aims which relate to your project. Don't write vague or general aims. You should **refer to aspects of your project** that you want to find out.

This is **specific** to the Research Study 'The Assassination of President John F. Kennedy, 1963'.

Make the aims your own by referring to information you want to find out.

> *Aims: My aims in doing this study are to explore the evidence in relation to Oswald, to examine theories about his motivation or the motivation of others, to review the conspiracies about the assassination and to assess the impact of the assassination. I want to read primary and secondary sources to understand different ideas about the assassination. There is so much bias and propaganda in relation to the assassination that trying to understand what happened will help develop my skills as an historian, which is another aim.*

3. Intended Approach: Here you state how you intend to research and complete your Research Study. **Refer to aspects of your project.**

> *Intended Approach: I have to be selective in my research because there are over 2,000 books on the Kennedy assassination. I will search for sources in my school and local county libraries, especially the reference section. I also intend to use the internet and to view the movie JFK by Oliver Stone, which hopefully should help with my research on the conspiracies. There are also some documentaries which may be of help. I want to read*

> *the more important secondary sources and use these to write up my research study. I will also evaluate them. I will consult my teacher and redraft my essay if necessary.*

4. Sources: Higher Level must list **three sources**, including the **work of an historian. Ordinary Level** must list **two sources.**

* Make sure your sources are listed at the *end of the page* on the Outline Plan, *not* in the Evaluation of Sources.
* Do not list any more than two (Ordinary Level) or three sources (Higher Level) because there are no marks for more than that.

When writing the Outline Plan and the Evaluation of Sources into the booklet:

* Use the full page down to the very end.
* Keep your writing clear.
* Reduce the size of your writing if it is usually large.

HOW TO LIST SOURCES

In previous exams, students have been given full marks for listing an author, title and some other information in relation to the publication, e.g. place of publication. As a general rule, **give as much information as possible about your sources** because the marking scheme can change from exam to exam.

Examples

Book

Author, title, publisher, place and date of publication:

James T. Patterson, *Grand Expectations, The United States, 1945–74*, Oxford University Press, Oxford, 1996.

Article

Author, title of article, title of magazine or journal, volume number and date of publication, page number:

Tim Clayton, 'Trafalgar, The Battle', *BBC History Magazine*, Vol. 6, No. 10, October 2005, pp. 14–17.

Internet

Title of website, internet address, author (or editors, if no author is given), date site was created, date you downloaded information:

Memorial and Museum, Auschwitz–Birkenau, http://www.auschwitz–muzeum. oswiecim.pl/html/eng/start/index.php, Editors: Teresa Swiebocka, Jaroslaw Mensfelt, 1999–2003, 13 October 2005.

Note: Do not list www.yahoo.com or www.google.com as sources. Give the full web address of the site you are using as a source.

TV/DVD Documentary

Title, TV channel (director, scriptwriter, narrator), date shown (month/year) or date created or produced (if you bought a DVD):

Dr Martin Luther King Jr., A Historical Perspective, written and directed by Thomas Friedman, Xenon Pictures, 2002. (Or if recorded from television, broadcast on The History Channel, 15 June 2007.)

Oral Sources

Interview, name of person, whether the person was a witness or participant, date of interview, notes and/or recording:

John Murphy, railway worker, witness to crash, interviewed on 12 January 2007, tape recording and notes.

Newspapers

Name of journalist (if given), title of article, name of paper, date, page number (if you have it):

Andrew Hamilton, 'Derry Prepares for "Siege of Stormont"', *The Irish Times*, Tuesday, 16 February 1965, p. 12.

Sources: (1) William D. Rubinstein, 'Oswald Shoots JFK' in History Today, Vol. 49, Issue 10, October 1999. (2) William Manchester, The Death of a President, Michael Joseph, London, 1967. (3) Gerald L. Posner, Case Closed: Lee Harvey Oswald and the Assasssination of JFK, Warner Bros, London, 1994.

Note: **Do not list** works of **historical fiction** (either books or films) in your sources – you could lose marks. For example: Even though I intend to view the film *JFK* for the Research Study on 'The Assassination of President John F. Kennedy, 1963', I will not list it as a source. I can **use** it and **refer** to it in my essay but I **will not list it** as a source. However, **documentary films** can be **listed** as sources.

EXAMPLES OF FINDING INFORMATION FOR LISTING BOOKS AND INTERNET SOURCES

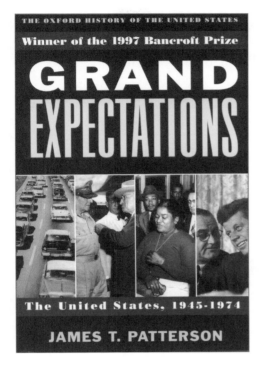

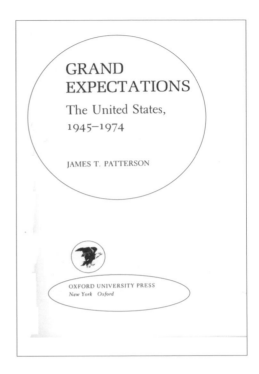

http://www.auschwitz.org.pl/new/index.php?language=EN&tryb=stale&d=434

File   Edit   View   Favorites   Tools   Help

:: Muzeum Auschwitz-Birkenau w Oświęcimiu EN ::

MEMORIAL AND MUSEUM
AUSCHWITZ-BIRKENAU

Technical page

Editors: Teresa Świebocka, Jarek Mensfelt.

Design: Krzysztof Antończyk, Ryszard Domasik, Marek Lach, Jarek Mensfelt.

Current photographs of the Auschwitz I and Auschwitz II-Birkenau sites: Ryszard Domasik, Marek Lach, Wojciech Gorgolewski, Jarek Mensfelt.

HTML editors: Marek Lach, Jarek Mensfelt.

Translated into English by: William Brand

Historical material based on "Auschwitz 1940-1945. Central Issues in the History of the Camp", published by the Museum.

Additional material based on the information tablets about the camp on the grounds of the Memorial.

Thanks to Wojciech Gorgolewski (gorpol@bci.krakow.pl) for providing current aerial photographs of Oswiecim.

We welcome your technical comments at:

muzeum@auschwitz.org.pl

History | Museum | Visiting the Memorial | Help | Bookshop | Latest News | Links | About the Site | Search | RSS |

Copyright ©1999-2007 Auschwitz-Birkenau State Museum, Poland
Since 2006-09-22 11:12:29 this page has been visited 6867 times.

PLEAN IMLÍNEACH (15 marc)
OUTLINE PLAN (15 marks)

Define and Justify: I intend to research the assassination of President John F. Kennedy (JFK) and the conspiracies which surrounded it since 1963. On 22 November 1963, JFK was fatally wounded in Dallas, Texas. The murder caused national uproar and since then Kennedy has become an icon of the 1960s. This topic is particularly significant because of the manner in which the most powerful political leader in a democratic country such as the US was killed, the controversy it provoked and the impact of Kennedy's death on the US. *Aims:* My aims in doing this study are to explore the evidence in relation to Oswald, to examine theories about his motivation or the motivation of others, to review the conspiracies about the assassination and to assess the impact of the assassination. I want to read primary and secondary sources to understand different ideas about the assassination. There is so much bias and propaganda in relation to the assassination that trying to understand what happened will help develop my skills as an historian, which is another aim.

Intended Approach: I have to be selective in my research because there are over 2,000 books on the Kennedy assassination. I will search for sources in my school and local county libraries, especially the reference section. I also intend to use the internet and to view the movie JFK by Oliver Stone, which hopefully should help with my research on the conspiracies. There are also some documentaries which may be of help. I want to read the more important secondary sources and use these to write up my research study. I will also evaluate them. I will consult my teacher and redraft my essay if necessary. **(9)**

Sources: (1) William D. Rubinstein, 'Oswald Shoots JFK' in History Today, Vol. 49, Issue 10, October 1999. (2) William Manchester, The Death of a President, Michael Joseph, London, 1967. (3) Gerald L. Posner, Case Closed: Lee Harvey Oswald and the Assasssination of JFK, Warner Bros, London, 1994. **(6)**

Include ubheadings

se the full page and keep the riting small

Evaluation of Sources (25 marks)

Writing the Evaluation of Sources

In the Evaluation of Sources, you must:

- Indicate the relevance of the sources to the subject.
- Comment on the **strengths** and **weaknesses** of the sources.

Your answer is marked on how well you do this 'clearly and coherently'.

> - Take notes on the Evaluation of Sources while you are using the source.
> - Do a final report on the Evaluation of Sources after you have finished the essay.

In **Higher Level**, the answer is graded from excellent (22–25 marks) to weak (0–8 marks). If you refer to only two sources, the maximum mark you can get is 17 marks, or a maximum of 9 marks if you only refer to one source.

In **Ordinary Level**, the answer is graded from very good (21–25 marks) to weak (0–7 marks) if you refer to both sources. If you refer to only one source, 17 marks is the maximum you can get.

In evaluating sources, refer to:

- **Relevance** of the sources to the topic – what did you find out about your Research Study from this source?
- **Strengths** and **weaknesses** of the sources – mention both strengths and weaknesses (at least one weakness).
- Mention **each of the sources** you have cited in your evaluation.
- **Vary your comments** for **each** evaluation.
- **Maximum** one A4 page – keep it concise.
- Use the **full page** when writing the evaluation.
- Keep your writing clear.
- Reduce the size of your writing if it is usually large.
- Do not waste space by repeating the full title and details of your sources here – the title of the article or book or the author's name will do, as you have listed them fully in the Outline Plan.

EVALUATING HISTORY BOOKS/ARTICLES

Apply **strengths and weaknesses** from the lists below to **evaluate your sources**.

Strengths:

- Places events in a wider context.
- Wide range of facts and information available on which to make a judgment.

- Uses primary and secondary sources.
- Can judge the influence/impact of events.
- Fair and balanced account.
- Analyses causes and consequences.
- Detailed and comprehensive account.
- Reputable author – see information in the textbook.
- Use of index and illustrations.

Weaknesses:
- Could be biased and/or biased author.
- Might not use wide range of primary and secondary sources. Might not provide any sources.
- No references.
- Could be used for propaganda.
- Limited, narrow account.
- Concentrated on one aspect only (name it).
- No index.
- No illustrations.

Note: When evaluating sources:
- Don't just give a general review. Make sure you **refer specifically** to information in your Research Study.
- Always link the strengths and weaknesses and key words **to the sources you used**, e.g. instead of saying 'The author interviewed many people', add on the name of somebody relevant to your project: 'The author interviewed President Kennedy's wife, Jacqueline.'

Use as many of these key words for the Evaluation of Sources as possible – mix them up between the different evaluations you have to do.
- Primary and secondary sources.
- Footnotes/notes.
- Bibliographical essay/bibliography.
- Index.
- Photographs.
- Reputation as an historian.
- Detailed and comprehensive.
- Explains.
- Describing.

- Placing it in its wider historical context.
- Style of writing.
- Analysing direct quotations.
- Interviewed many of the people.
- Narrative account.
- Biased/unbiased version.
- Balanced and fair/one-sided account.
- Objective/selective.
- Well written.
- Plenty/too much information.
- Too many or too few figures/graphs/maps.
- Used primary and/or secondary sources.
- Very difficult reading.
- Use of technical jargon.
- Not enough detail/too much detail.
- Well illustrated (especially if a magazine).

Some things to watch out for when you are evaluating a book:

- Well laid out contents.

- Footnotes (or notes at the end of the book).

Contents

Editor's Introduction   xvii

Prologue: August 1945   3

1. Veterans, Ethnics, Blacks, Women   10
2. Unions, Liberals, and the State: Stalemate   39
3. Booms   61
4. Grand Expectations About the World   82
5. Hardening of the Cold War, 1945–1948   105
6. Domestic Politics: Truman's First Term   137
7. Red Scares Abroad and at Home   165
8. Korea   207
9. Ike   243
10. World Affairs, 1953–1956   276
11. The Biggest Boom Yet   311
12. Mass Consumer Culture   343
13. Race   375

1940s, which ultimately threw millions of farm laborers out of work, and in part to the opening up of industrial employment in the North during the wartime boom, roughly a million blacks (along with even more whites) moved from the South during the 1940s. Another 1.5 million Negroes left the South in the 1950s. This was a massive migration in so short a time—one of the most significant demographic shifts in American history—and it was often agonizingly stressful.[22] The black novelist Ralph Ellison wrote in 1952 of the hordes of blacks who "shot up from the South into the busy city like wild jacks-in-the-box broken loose from our springs—so sudden that our gait becomes like that of deep-sea divers suffering from the bends."[23]

Still, many of the migrants gradually reaped unprecedented benefits. The number of Negroes employed in manufacturing jumped from 500,000 to 1.2 million during the war. The percentage of employed black women who worked as domestic servants—before the war one of the few jobs they could get—declined from 72 to 48 during the same period. Blacks also advanced on other fronts, which seem token in retrospect but represented notable achievements at the time. In 1944 for the first time a black reporter was admitted to a presidential press conference; in 1947 blacks gained access at last to the Senate press gallery.[24] Thanks in part to legal pressure from the National Association for the Advancement of Colored People (NAACP), the Supreme Court in 1944 outlawed the "white primary," a ploy that had enabled states in the South to exclude blacks from all-important Democratic primary races.[25] In 1946 the Court

22. Nicholas Lemann, *The Promised Land: The Great Black Migration and How It Changed America* (New York, 1991).
23. Ralph Ellison, *Invisible Man* (New York, 1952), 332.
24. Harvard Sitkoff, *The Struggle for Black Equality, 1954–1992* (New York, 1993), 3–19; Manning Marable, *Race, Reform, and Rebellion: The Second Reconstruction in Black America, 1945–1990* (Jackson, 1991), 13–39; David Goldfield, *Black, White, and Southern: Race Relations and Southern Culture, 1940 to the Present* (Baton Rouge, 1990), 45–62; and William Harris, *The Harder We Run: Black Workers Since the Civil War* (New York, 1982), 123–89, are four of many books that deal in part with postwar race relations. See also James Jones, *Bad Blood: The Tuskegee Experiment, a Tragedy of Race and Medicine* (New York, 1981), for a particularly egregious story of racist science.
25. *Smith v. Allwright*, 321 U.S. 649 (1944).

- Bibliography.

Information such as this can be useful in your evaluation, but make it **relevant to your Research Study.**

Bibliographical Essay

As footnotes in the text suggest, the literature concerning postwar United States history is vast. This brief bibliographical essay mentions only those books that proved most useful to me. It begins by identifying general interpretations of the era as well as sources concerned with various themes and topics: race relations, religion, the economy, and so on. The bibliography then follows the chronological organization of the chapters, referring to books (for articles, see footnotes) that deal with particular time periods and controversies, beginning with the Truman era and concluding with sources in the early 1970s.

General interpretations: Among the best books that seek to make sense of this era are William Chafe, *The Unfinished Journey: America Since World War II* (New York, 1991), an especially well written and well argued survey; John Blum, *Years of Discord: American Politics and Society, 1961–1974* (New York, 1991); John Diggins, *The Proud Decades: America in War and Peace, 1941–1960* (New York, 1988); Steve Fraser and Gary Gerstle, eds., *The Rise and Fall of the New Deal Order, 1930–1980* (Princeton, 1989), a collection of articles focusing on labor and politics; Godfrey Hodgson, *America in Our Time* (Garden City, N.Y., 1976); William Leuchtenburg, *In the Shadow of F.D.R.: From Harry Truman to Ronald Reagan* (Ithaca, 1983); Leuchtenburg, *A Troubled Feast: American Society since 1945* (Boston, 1973); Alonzo Hamby, *Liberalism and Its Challengers: From F.D.R. to Bush* (New York, 1992), a book of informed essays on major political figures; Marty Jezer, *The Dark Ages: Life in the United States, 1945–1960* (Boston, 1982), a critical account; William O'Neill, *American High: The Years of Confidence, 1945–1960* (New York, 1986), which presents a very different view from Jezer's; James Sundquist, *Politics and Policy: The Eisenhower, Kennedy, and Johnson Years* (Washington, 1968), a still useful analysis of public programs; Morris Janowitz, *The Last Half-Century: Societal Change and Politics in America* (Chicago, 1978), which is informative on social trends; Alan Wolfe, *America's Impasse: The Rise and Fall of the Politics of Growth* (New York, 1981); Wolfe, ed., *America at Century's End* (Berkeley, 1991), an especially strong collection of topical essays on trends since World War II; and Frederick Siegel, *Troubled Journey: From Pearl Harbor to Ronald Reagan* (New York, 1984). Important books offering interpretive surveys of postwar foreign policies are John Gaddis, *Strategies of Containment: A*

791

HISTORY

Winner of the 1997 Bancroft Prize in History

In *Grand Expectations*, James T. Patterson has written a highly readable and balanced work that weaves the major political, cultural, and economic events of the period into a superb portrait of America from 1945 through Watergate. Here is an era teeming with memorable events—from the bloody campaigns in Korea and the bitterness surrounding McCarthyism to the assassinations of the Kennedys and Martin Luther King, to the Vietnam War and Nixon's resignation in 1974. Patterson excels at portraying the amazing growth after World War II as well as the resultant buoyancy of spirit. And he shows how this upbeat, can-do mood spurred grander and grander expectations as the era progressed.

Of course, not all Americans shared in this economic growth, and an important thread running through the book is an informed and gripping depiction of the civil rights movement—from the electrifying *Brown v. Board of Education* decision, to the violent confrontations in Little Rock, Birmingham, and Selma, to the landmark civil rights acts of 1964 and 1965. Patterson also shows how the Vietnam War and a growing rights revolution triggered a backlash. And by Nixon's resignation, we find a national mood in contrast to the grand expectations of ten years earlier, one in which faith in our leaders and in the attainability of the American dream was becoming shaken.

Grand Expectations is a brilliant summation of the years that created the America that we know today, a time of setbacks amid unmatched and lasting achievements.

"A magisterial history. . . . A fair, judicious, and yet decisive synthesis."   *Atlantic Monthly*

"A spirited, sprawling narrative of American life."   *The New York Times Book Review*

"A *tour de force* from the last murmurings of the New Deal through the last mutterings over Watergate."   *The Wall Street Journal*

"With unassuming virtuosity, James T. Patterson succeeds brilliantly at every turn in *Grand Expectations*. . . . One can hardly imagine a better overview of American life during the Cold War, the struggle for civil rights, and the debacle of Vietnam."   *The Washington Post Book World*

James T. Patterson is Ford Foundation Professor of History at Brown University.

Cover photographs, left to right: Superstock; Library of Congress; AP/Library of Congress; UPI/Bettmann

Cover design by David Tran

Oxford Paperbacks
Oxford University Press
U.S. $26.00

ISBN 978-0-19-511797-4

9 780195 117974   90000

EVALUATING INTERNET SOURCES

Apply **strengths and weaknesses** from the list below to evaluate your sources.

> - **Make it your own:** Apply these ideas to the internet source you used. Use information relevant to your Research Study, e.g. if you wrote that 'the site uses many primary sources', give an *example* of one of these. Or if you think it is a reputable site, say *why*.

Strengths:

- Uses many primary sources, both written documents and visual sources.
- Uses many secondary articles.

- Is a reputable site, e.g. archives, universities, libraries.
- Easily accessed.
- Signed by author, notes cited.
- Also use relevant strengths from the history book/articles list on pp. 10–11.

Weaknesses:

- Biased.
- Used for propaganda.
- Information not reliably researched and checked.
- Author unknown or not identified.
- Also use relevant weaknesses from the history book/articles list on pp. 10–11.

Some things to watch out for when evaluating an internet source:

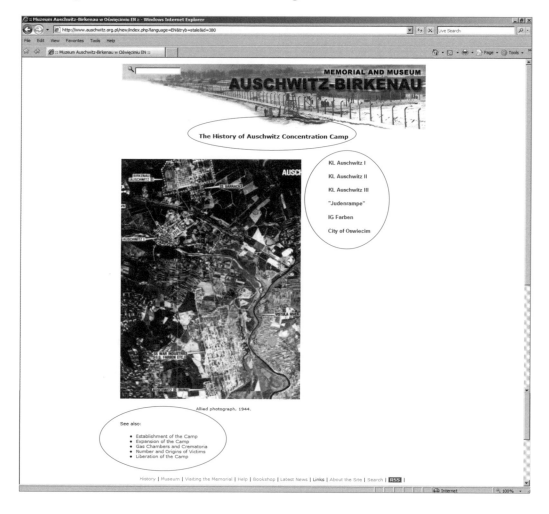

EXAMPLE – HOW TO USE RELEVANT PHRASES IN AN EVALUATION OF A SOURCE

Some or all of these phrases can be used to write up an evaluation. Don't write a general evaluation – make it **specific to the book/article/internet site** you have used.

- Places events in a wider context.
- Wide range of facts and information available on which to make a judgment.
- Uses primary and secondary sources.
- Can judge the influence/impact of events.
- Fair and balanced account.
- Analyses causes and consequences.
- Detailed and comprehensive account.
- Reputable author.
- Use of index and illustrations/graphics.

Example – Evaluation of Source

Gerald Posner's *Case Closed* is a detailed analysis of the events, personalities and conspiracies surrounding the assassination of President Kennedy. In a fair and balanced account, he draws on a wide range of facts and information to investigate the life and character of Lee Harvey Oswald, the trajectory of the three shots, especially the magic bullet which went through Kennedy into Connally, and Oswald's escape route. The detailed graphics illustrating these were particularly helpful. Posner supports the Warren Commission and the view that Oswald shot Kennedy. He is a reputable author who uses his legal training to dissect the evidence. He backs up his conclusions with over seventy pages of notes and a large bibliography of primary and secondary sources. It is difficult to find a weakness in this book, except that because of the huge amount of detail I could not read the entire book and I may have missed some key points.

Can you identify the strengths, weaknesses and relevance in the evaluation above? The title of the Research Study is 'The Assassination of President John F. Kennedy, 1963'.

A COMPLETED EVALUATION OF SOURCES

MEASTÓIREACHT AR NA FOINSÍ (25 MARC)
EVALUATION OF THE SOURCES (25 MARKS)

Only use title or author

(1) *'Oswald Shoots JFK'* is a detailed and informative account of the events of 22 November 1963. It provides background information on Lee Harvey Oswald and details of the assassination. It reviews the workings of the Warren Commission and the various conspiracy theories. The author, a professor of Modern History in the University of Wales, shows wide knowledge of the topic. He favours the Warren Commission but he suggests a new motive for Oswald's killings: that Kennedy was not the target, Connally was. However, since this is an article in a magazine it is not long enough for the author to give enough detail to support his views. (2) *Manchester's book* is a very comprehensive account of almost 800 pages. It deals not only with the events surrounding the assassination, but also with President Kennedy's funeral in Washington. There is an extensive index and many primary and secondary sources are listed in the bibliography, including almost 350 interviews. There are also useful maps of the main locations. The book is too long, but I got enough information from the detailed account of the assassination. One weakness is that he doesn't use any footnotes, so his statements are not supported directly. He says he is not biased, but he was asked to write the book by Jacqueline Kennedy. (3) *Gerald Posner's Case Closed* is a detailed analysis of the events, personalities and conspiracies surrounding the assassination of President Kennedy. In a fair and balanced account, he draws on a wide range of facts and information to investigate the life and character of Lee Harvey Oswald, the trajectory of the three shots, especially the magic bullet which went through Kennedy into Connally, and Oswald's escape route. Posner supports the Warren Commission in the view that Oswald shot Kennedy. He is a reputable author who backs up his conclusions with over seventy pages of notes and a large bibliography of primary and secondary sources. It is difficult to find a weakness in this book, except that because of the huge amount of details, I could not read the entire book and I may have missed some key points.

Keep the same order as your list of sources in the Outline Plan

Use the full page

The Extended Essay (60 marks)

The Extended Essay has two parts:

- Main findings and conclusions of the Research Study, written with an introduction, paragraphs, conclusion; line of logical development (50 marks).
- A Review of the Research Process undertaken and the success in achieving the aims of the Outline Plan (10 marks).

Total words for the Extended Essay, including the Review of the Research process = 1200–1500 words (Higher Level).

- Research essay = 1250–1300 words.
- Review of the Process = 200–250 words.

Ordinary Level = 600–800 words.

- Research essay = 675–700 words.
- Review of the Process = 100–125 words.

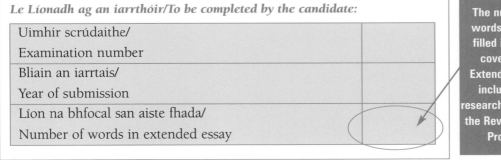

Le Líonadh ag an iarrthóir/To be completed by the candidate:		The number of words must be filled in on the cover – the Extended Essay includes the research essay and the Review of the Process.
Uimhir scrúdaithe/ Examination number		
Bliain an iarrtais/ Year of submission		
Líon na bhfocal san aiste fhada/ Number of words in extended essay		

Features of the Extended Essay:

- Word processing software will give you the word count.
- Check spelling and grammar. Watch out for Americanisation of the spelling.
- Use paragraphs.
- Full introduction and conclusion.
- Use a quote(s).
- Mention an historian.
- Length – about five to six pages, depending on the size of the handwriting.

Quotes:

- If you are quoting directly from a source, use quotation marks.

- At the end of the quote, you can decide whether or not to include the author's name in brackets, e.g. (Rubenstein).
- If you want to identify the quote, use one of the three sources you have listed in the outline plan.

CRITERIA USED FOR MARKING THE RESEARCH ESSAY (50 MARKS)

The research essay is marked under three headings:
1. Presentation.
2. Research skills.
3. Historical knowledge.

Show evidence of each of these in the main findings and conclusion of the research essay.

1. Presentation (10 marks):
- Literacy.
- Structure.
- Coherence.

So far there have been no marks deducted for excessive length, but it could happen, so if you go over the limit, don't go too far.

2. Research skills (15 marks):
- Appropriate depth of investigation.
- Use of sources.
- Fair and balanced treatment of issues.

3. Historical knowledge (25 marks):
- Thorough.
- Accurate.
- Relevant to title.

Other possible criteria:
- Broader historical context – link to wider historical issues.
- Provisional nature of historical knowledge.
- Historians' changing views on your topic, e.g. new evidence.

WRITING THE REVIEW OF THE PROCESS (10 MARKS)

* Keep the Review separate.
* The Review should be approximately 250 words. (About one page of handwriting.)
* Put the Review at the beginning or end of the Extended Essay. (Better at the end.)
* Use a heading, such as 'The Review of the Research Process'.
* Refer back to the Aims of the Outline Plan – did you achieve them? Explain briefly.
* Include references to **information found out or not found out** about your project.
* Use **relevant** ideas, rephrase where necessary and refer to success/failure in achieving the Aims of the Outline Plan.

In writing the Review of the Process, use some of the following words/phrases:

consulted teacher, developed outline plan, read the sources, took notes, extracted the key information, identified bias, sorted out causes and effects, evaluated the sources, used the internet, visited libraries, compared the information, planned the structure of my report, with an introduction, paragraphs and a conclusion, one main idea for each paragraph, difficulty condensing all the information into a short essay, tried to be fair and objective, re-drafted the report, failed to get certain information, would have liked to write more/find out more about, libraries helpful/unhelpful, internet very good/flawed/inaccurate, process of historical research, skills of historian.

> Make it your own: Make it specific to your Research Study by referring to information in your work, libraries you used, experiences you had, etc.

Example

Reword the following paragraph so that you can give information relevant to your Research Study.

I got the idea of my research study from …… The research I undertook helped to develop my research skills (*any example*) …… We do not have a school library (or very few books in the school library on my topic) …… I had never used the (*name of the*) county library before …… The county library was better than the city library for my sources (*or the opposite*) …… I looked up the library catalogue on the internet (*give the internet address*) …… I used a microfilm reader for the first time …… I used an inter-library loan to get a book (*from*) …… Could not find some sources (*example*) ...... I had difficulties ...... (*such as* ......) Also, I had never used the internet to research a topic in history ......   (*any other sources used by you?*) I interviewed ...... I had to undertake most of the work on my own ...... I had to decide between information in different sources (*any example?*)...... I learned a great deal about note–taking and using the notes in writing the report. I consulted my teacher about the Outline Plan and about sources. I had to learn about the report structure in providing an introduction, paragraphs and a conclusion. My teacher reviewed the drafts of my research study ...... I had to redraft because ...... I had to condense information because ...... I had to ensure my report was fair and objective. I had to reword some sentences ...... I achieved most of my aims; in particular, I found out about ...... (*or did not find out about* ......) By the end of the research study, I had a much clearer idea about the work of the historian and the process of historical research ...... (*especially, give an example* ......) I am glad I choose this topic because ......

SUMMARY

Draft:

- Draft your answers for the Outline Plan, Evaluation of Sources and the Review of the Research Process.
- **Make it your own**: Make as many references as possible to your own Research Study.

Practice:

- Practise your answers on **blank pages** of the Research Study booklet (History Coursework Journal), available at www.examinations.ie.

Keep to the length (approx.):

- Keep your essay length to 1250–1300 words. (Higher Level)
- Keep the Review of the Research Process to 200–250 words.

CHECKLIST

Have you all of the following? ✓ **Tick each box.**

1. Title – does the title fit the content?   ☐
2. Have you completed the Outline Plan?   ☐

3. Have you listed three sources at the bottom of the outline plan (Higher Level)? ☐

4. Have you included a source from an historian in the list? ☐

5. Have you evaluated three sources? ☐

6. Have you included strengths and weaknesses for each source? ☐

7. Have you included the relevance of the source to the Research Study? ☐

8. Have you completed the Extended Essay with a maximum of 1500 words (research essay + review) for Higher Level? ☐

9. Have you included a Review of the Process? ☐

10. Did you refer back to the Aims of the Outline Plan? ☐

Example of an Extended Essay

THE RESEARCH ESSAY

Ensure your title fits the essay. Change the title if you have to.

The Assassination of President John F. Kennedy, 1963

'For all in whose hearts he still lives – a watchman of honour who never sleeps.'

President John F. Kennedy was assassinated in Dallas, Texas in November 1963. His assassination had a profound effect on affluent, optimistic America. His position as one of the most powerful men in the world, his image as a charismatic, dynamic young leader, the belief in the American Dream, the death of the alleged assassin so soon afterwards, the failure to provide immediate answers for the public and the influence of the mass media all contributed to the spread of conspiracy theories in relation to his death. In turn, these theories became a symptom of the widespread doubt and scepticism that began to spread in America.

Keep background material to the introduction

The immediate circumstances of the assassination are well known. Three years into his term as president, JFK was trying to increase his support for the upcoming elections in 1964. As part of this campaign, Kennedy went to Dallas, Texas, accompanied by Vice-President Johnson and their wives. Texas had a Democratic governor, John Connally, but the Republican Party had been attracting more support there. Johnson, a Texan himself, had visited Texas previously to promote

Historical context

the Democratic campaign but had been faced with hostile reactions from demonstrators.

The presidential party flew into Dallas on Friday, 22 November 1963. On the way to a civic luncheon, the car drove down Main Street towards a valley beneath a railway bridge; a six-storey building named the Texas Schoolbook Depository overlooked the road. A protective, bullet-proof plexiglas had been removed from Kennedy's car at his own request so he could wave to well-wishers and so the people of Dallas could see the vote-winning First Lady. The car was just passing the Texas Schoolbook Depository building when shots were fired, fatally wounding President Kennedy and seriously injuring John Connally.

Almost immediately after the shooting, the President's car accelerated to Parkland Memorial Hospital, where surgeons fought to save his life, but shortly after his admittance to Parkland, the President died. A brief argument followed this between Kennedy's staff and Dallas police over possession of the body. Eventually, it was placed in a casket for the flight back to Washington. Vice-President Johnson was designated to succeed Kennedy and was sworn in as President as Air Force One left Dallas. Shortly after, he set up the Warren Commission to 'ascertain, evaluate and report upon the facts relating to the assassination of the late President John F. Kennedy.'

Historians have called the assassination of President Kennedy 'one of the watershed events of the twentieth century' and also 'one of contemporary history's most enduring mysteries'. But the Warren Commission, reporting after a ten-month investigation, was definite in its conclusions. It stated that:

- The shots which killed President Kennedy and wounded Governor Connally were fired from the sixth-floor window of the south-east corner of the Texas Schoolbook Depository.
- There were only three shots fired and these were fired by Lee Harvey Oswald.
- There was no evidence that Lee Harvey Oswald or Jack Ruby, who killed Oswald two days later, were part of any conspiracy, domestic or foreign, to assassinate President Kennedy.
- The Commission concluded that Lee Harvey Oswald acted alone.

The evidence against Oswald was clear cut. His palm print was found on the Mannlicher-Carcano rifle which fired the shots. His fingerprints were found on book

Use shor quote(s) – role o evidence

cartons and a brown paper bag. Witnesses testified seeing him on the sixth floor at the time, and one claimed he saw him with a rifle at the window. He purchased the rifle under the name of A.J. Hiddell and he owned the post office box – 2915 – where it was sent. However, many people did not believe that this was the case. They asked how Kennedy's assassination could be carried out 'by a maladjusted loner with a mail-order rifle'.

Even before the Warren Commission reported, conspiracy theories and alternative explanations began to surface and became more widespread as the years went on. Some claimed that the Mafia were responsible for the assassination of Kennedy, using Ruby's connection with the Mafia to support this. This theory was based on the idea that the Mafia were angry with both John F. Kennedy and Robert Kennedy for their attempts to destroy the gangsters. C. Robert Blakey, chief counsel and staff director to the House Select Committee on Assassinations from 1977 to 1979, published The Plot to Kill the President in 1981. In the book, Blakey argues that Lee Harvey Oswald was involved but believed that there was a second gunman firing from a 'grassy knoll' in front of the President's car. Blakey came to the conclusion that Mafia boss Carlos Marcello organised the assassination. The 1988 television documentary, The Men Who Killed Kennedy, also supported the Mafia theory but blamed it on the Marseilles Mafia.

Other conspiracy theories refer to the role of the Central Intelligence Agency (CIA) and the Federal Bureau of Investigation (FBI). Some claimed that J. Edgar Hoover, head of the FBI, believed that Kennedy would force him into retirement when he reached seventy. They suggested that Hoover himself either knew of the plans to kill Kennedy and did nothing to stop them or helped to organise the assassination. Others said that CIA agents worked on behalf of a 'high cabal' of industrialists and bankers. Finally, Anthony Summers, in The Kennedy Conspiracy, linked the CIA with his view that Kennedy was killed by anti-Castro activists funded by the Mafia, who had been forced out of Cuba.

One of the theories has been given more publicity than others, and that is the belief of Jim Garrison, the District Attorney of New Orleans. He believed that a group of right-wing activists were involved in a conspiracy with the CIA. His views were the basis of Oliver Stone's movie, JFK. Many witnesses supported Stone's contentions. Observers felt that it was a major cover-up, with many questions being asked about

> **Be fair minded and unbiased in the use of language**

the lost interrogation notes of Will Fritz, the policeman who arrested Oswald, and the subsequent deaths and disappearances in the case.

Many other theories have been put forward to explain the assassination of JFK. Not surprisingly, given the Cold War and the Cuban Missile Crisis, some believed that Khrushchev and the Soviet Union were behind it. This was linked to Oswald's time in that country. Others have blamed Lyndon Johnson and Texas oil millionaires. However, all the alternative theorists have failed to provide definite evidence for their views. Many of the theories were put together by amateur historians who made no systematic investigation of the evidence. But they did have a profound effect on the public perception of the assassination. By the late 1980s, opinion polls showed that 80 per cent of Americans did not believe the conclusions of the Warren Commission.

The death of JFK still remains a mystery. However, more recent investigations have favoured the work of the Warren Commission, particularly Gerald Posner's Case Closed: Lee Harvey Oswald and the Assassination of JFK. He researched all claims by critics of the Warren Commission and refuted each one. However, the problem of motivation still remains – Oswald had no known grievance against Kennedy. But as Professor Rubenstein points out, he did have a grievance against Connally. If this is the case, and Connally rather than Kennedy was the target, then all the conspiracy theories are wrong.

Whatever the truth about Kennedy's assassination, his death has also caused debate over its impact and his legacy. Some have argued that his death led to America's disastrous involvement in Vietnam. They have suggested that his second term would have seen progress in domestic policies such as civil rights. Other historians have claimed that John F. Kennedy was a mediocre president. 'Had he obtained a second term, federal civil rights policy during the 1960s would have been substantially less productive and US actions in Vietnam no different from what actually occurred. His tragic assassination was not a tragedy for the course of American history.' But it still provokes controversy.

The Review of the Process

After my history teacher viewed my Outline Plan, I began my research. This plan was extremely useful to me in guiding my work. The computer teacher gave me

Views c
historiar

permission to use the computer rooms in my school, where I was able to print off articles from the main internet sites. However, the majority of these were unsatisfactory, being contradictory and biased, so I visited libraries to find more suitable sources. My school library had no books on the Kennedy assassination, but I found relevant books in the county library (www.corkcoco.ie) and the UCC library (www.ucc.ie), including a reprint of the findings of the Warren Commission Report.

I first read all my sources and took relevant notes from each. I found an extremely useful article in a history magazine and photocopied the parts I needed, as I had to return it. I contacted video stores in order to locate JFK by Oliver Stone. I also saw a BBC documentary, Oswald's Ghost, which helped me understand what happened, especially by showing film shot at the time. I compared my sources in order to ensure my project was as accurate as possible. Manchester's book was helpful if I had a doubt. I then planned the proper structure, including an introduction, paragraphs and a conclusion. I used one theme for each paragraph, such as 'The Impact/Effects', and wrote all the relevant details under that theme. I used information from my sources to support each paragraph. I am convinced that Oswald alone shot Kennedy, but I'm still not sure why he did it. I tried to remain objective throughout, although I had difficulty shortening my essay to the recommended limit. I was satisfied I achieved my Aims and had a much better understanding of the Kennedy assassination and the controversy surrounding it.

Part of this research was done in class, where I had the opportunity to question my teacher. Doing this project helped me to not only develop my research skills, it also gave me an ability to think independently. I had to undertake most of this research on my own. I became very much aware of how bias influences people. Most of the conspiracy theories were so far-fetched it was easy to dismiss them. I learned a great deal about taking notes and also how to lay out a proper structure when doing essays in History. By the end of the project I had a much clearer idea of the work of the historian and the process of historical research. I was glad I picked this project because it increased my interest in America.

Signing off:

- When you have written up your Research Study into the official booklet provided by the Department of Education and Science, your teacher will ask you to sign a form which says that the Research Study is your own work.
- The teacher and school principal will also sign the form.
- You will also be given a plastic envelope, which you will place your Research Study into and write your examination number on.
- This will be held in the school until the final History examination in June. You will then be asked to place your examination paper in that envelope as well.

Marking Scheme: Research Study (Higher Level)

OUTLINE PLAN (15 MARKS)

Citation of the sources = 6 marks.
Other elements = 9 marks.

Citation of sources:

- Three appropriate sources are asked for.
- Accurate citation of each appropriate source = 2 marks.
- Always give the **full reference** for your sources, e.g. for a book list the author, title, publisher, place and date of publication (see pp. 5–6).

Author + title only = 1 mark.
Extra item of validating information (e.g. publisher, date) = 1 mark.
2 marks x 3 = max 6 marks for three sources.

N.B. 'Standard school text books will not be regarded as suitable sources for the purposes of the Research Study'. – DES/NCCA *Guidelines*, p. 14.

Define and justify the proposed subject of study, identifying the aims and intended approach:

- Does the candidate clearly set out what it is he/she proposes to study and why? Does the candidate set out his/her aims and how he/she hopes to achieve those?
- Under the three criteria, to what extent does the candidate succeed in doing this clearly and coherently?

Define and Justify	*Identify Aims*	*Identify Approach*
(max = 3 marks)	(max = 3 marks)	(max = 3 marks)
Very good = 3	Very good = 3	Very good = 3
Good = 2	Good = 2	Good = 2
Fair = 1	Fair = 1	Fair = 1

EVALUATION OF THE SOURCES (25 MARKS)

- Comment on the strengths and/or weaknesses of sources and indicate the relevance of sources to the subject.
- To what extent does the candidate succeed in doing this clearly and coherently?

Reference to all three sources	*Reference to only two sources*	*Reference to only one source*
Excellent = 22–25 marks	Excellent = 15–17 marks	Excellent = 8–9 marks
Very good = 17–21 marks	Very good = 12–14 marks	Very good = 6–7 marks
Good = 13–16 marks	Good = 9–11 marks	Good = 4–5 marks
Fair = 9–12 marks	Fair = 6–8 marks	Fair = 2–3 marks
Weak = 0–8 marks	Weak = 0–5 marks	Weak = 0–1 marks

EXTENDED ESSAY (60 MARKS)

- Historical essay = 50 marks.
- Review of Research Process = 10 marks.
- The Review of the Research Process may be integral to the essay or presented as a separate element.
- The historical essay should be assessed as a unit and a mark out of 50, awarded as follows.

Historical knowledge (25 marks)	Excellent: 21–25
	Very good: 16–20
	Good: 11–15
	Fair: 6–10
	Weak: 0–5

Research skills (15 marks)	Excellent: 13–15
	Very good: 10–12
	Good: 7–9
	Fair: 4–6
	Weak: 0–3

Presentation (10 marks)	Excellent: 9–10
	Very good: 7–8
	Good: 5–6
	Fair: 3–4
	Weak: 0–2

Section 2
Document-based Case Studies

Document-based Case Studies

Leaving Cert Examination 2008 and 2009

The USA and the World, 1945–89

      The Montgomery Bus Boycott, 1955–56

      Lyndon Johnson and Vietnam, 1963–68

      The Moon Landing, 1969

Leaving Cert Examination 2010 and 2011

Politics and Society in Northern Ireland, 1949–93

      The Coleraine University Controversy

      The Apprentice Boys of Derry

      The Sunningdale Agreement and the Power-sharing Executive, 1973–74

Guidelines for Answering Document-based Questions

The document-based Case Studies will be examined in a question with the following format:

	Ordinary Level	Higher Level (marks)
1. Comprehension	40	20
2. Comparison	20	20
3. Criticism	20	20
4. Contextualiation	20	40

Guidelines for Answering Document Questions

1. Comprehension: Extract relevant data from documents to answer questions.

- **Underline the relevant parts of the extract, give full answers – quote from the documents (A, B and C, if there are three documents).**

Type of questions:

In Document A, mention two ways …… what is meant by ……? According to Document A, how/why/what/when ……? What is the message of the cartoon in Document B? What evidence does Document B offer about ……?

2. Comparison: Compare two or more accounts of the same historical experience and note similarities and contrasts.

- **Use both documents – compare one with the other – give a number of points in both parts of the question, (a) and (b).**

Type of questions:

Which document contains only facts …… (both facts and opinions)? Which document is more sympathetic to ……? How do the documents differ in their interpretation of ……? Which document is a personal account? Which document is more effective in communicating its message/making its point? Comment on the portrayal of …… in documents A and B. Which document …… agrees with ……? Mention one way in which Document A agrees/disagrees with …… How does Document A differ from Document B in relation to ……?

3. Criticism: Be able to recognise bias and propaganda; note viewpoint; identify contradictions; make judgments about the reliability of various sources.

- **Learn notes on strengths and weaknesses of main sources – know difference between eyewitness accounts, newspapers, public (government) records/reports, memoirs, diaries, letters, photographs, cartoons, etc. – use evidence from both documents, A/B (and C).**
- **Know objective, subjective, biased, balanced view, reliable, fact/opinion, propaganda, strengths/weaknesses as historical sources, primary/secondary source, viewpoint, perspective, provenance (origin of document).**

Type of questions:

Do you find bias in either document? How reliable is Document A ......? What are the strengths and weaknesses of ...... as an historical source? Which is of greater use to the historian ......? Mention two features of Document A that are characteristic of a newspaper report. Is Document A a primary source or a secondary source? Mention one strength and one weakness of Document A as a primary/secondary source. In relation to Document B, can you identify one of the following: bias, objectivity, reliability? Do you agree that the historian would need to use both documents to achieve a balanced view of ......?

4. Contextualisation: Place the subject matter of the documents in their historical context and show understanding of issues and events associated with that period.

- **Keep to the question asked – about two A4 pages with introduction, paragraphs, conclusion – use link sentences in the paragraphs – write like a mini-essay.**

Type of questions:

How did ...... deal with the difficulties ......? What are ...... strengths and weaknesses as a ......? How did ...... between ...... and ......? Describe the ...... up to ...... Did ...... achieve its aims during the period ......? What impact did ...... have during the period ......? What was the importance of ......?

Note: There is a danger of spending too much time on the Document question. Keep to the time – no more than forty-five minutes.

THE UNITED STATES AND THE WORLD, 1945–89

A Framework for the Case Studies

Each of the Case Studies has links to Elements in the Topics. It is important to study *both* the relevant Elements as well as the Case Study.

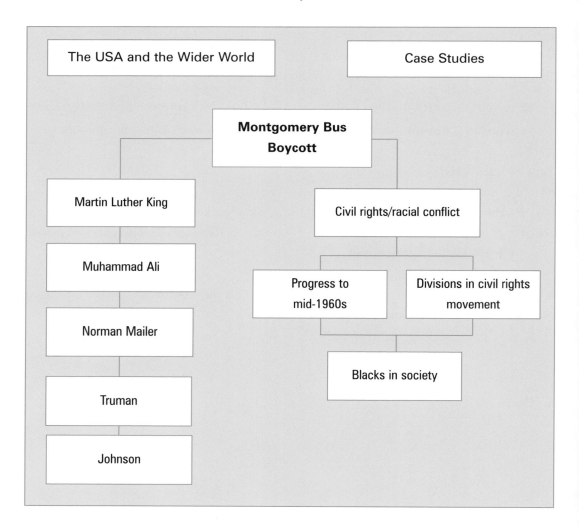

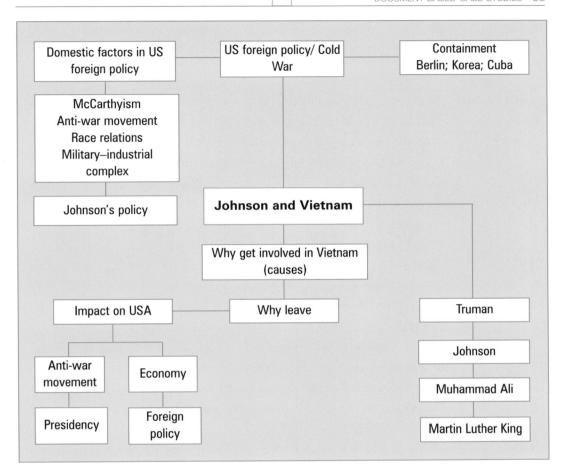

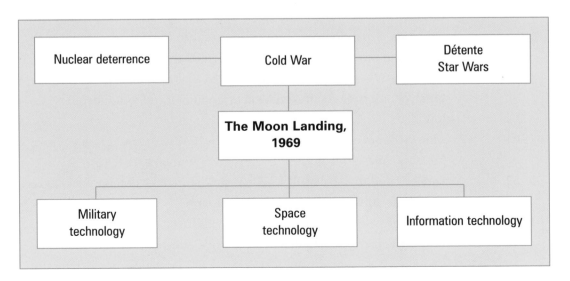

CIVIL RIGHTS IN THE US – TIMELINE

19th century   American Civil War ended; slavery abolished, but southern US states used Jim Crow laws to segregate (separate) blacks and whites.

1945   Post-war America – discrimination against blacks continued, especially in the South; the NAACP (National Association for the Advancement of Colored People) and CORE (Congress for Racial Equality) were fighting for black civil rights.

1948   President Truman issued executive order to end segregation in the US armed forces.

1953   Chief Justice Earl Warren appointed to the US Supreme court; chief justice until 1969.

1954   *Brown v. The Board of Education, Topeka, Kansas*; Supreme Court found that segregated public schools were unconstitutional.

1955–56   The Montgomery Bus Boycott – Rosa Parks refused to give up her seat to a white passenger; Montgomery Improvement Association (MIA) organised a bus boycott which lasted for almost a year and brought Martin Luther King to prominence; segregated bus system declared unconstitutional.

1957   Martin Luther King founded the Southern Christian Leadership Conference, which advocated non-violent protest. Federal troops used to protect black students entering Central High School in Little Rock, Arkansas. Civil Rights Commission set up by US government to investigate places where blacks were denied the vote.

1960   The Lunch Counter protests organised by black students to desegregate lunch counters. Student Non-Violent Coordinating Committee (SNCC) founded.

1961   The Freedom Rides were organised by CORE (Congress for Racial Equality) and SNCC to test desegregation in interstate buses.

1962   James Meredith, a black air force veteran, received federal protection to attend the all-white University of Mississippi.

1963   Civil rights organisers used schoolchildren as demonstrators in Birmingham, Alabama; attacked by white police. Martin Luther King gave his 'I have a dream speech' before 250,000 people in Washington.

1964	Martin Luther King awarded the Nobel Peace Prize. The Civil Rights Act passed, which outlawed discrimination in public places, including restaurants, theatres, sport stadiums and cinemas.
1965	Malcolm X, a black nationalist leader, assassinated. Selma to Birmingham March to protest over voting discrimination against blacks. The Voting Rights Act passed, which gave power to the federal government over voter registration. President Johnson used affirmative action to ensure government contractors employ minority workers. Rise of Black Power opposed to non-violent strategy of Martin Luther King.
1965–68	Race riots in cities ranging from Los Angeles to Harlem, New York and Chicago.
1968	The assassination of Martin Luther King in Memphis, Tennessee. American Indian Movement (AIM) founded.

Case Study: The Montgomery Bus Boycott, 1955–56

SAMPLE QUESTION 1

Document A

A protest against Jim Crow laws.

Jim Crow laws in practice.

Source: Jim Crow Must Go, Bruce Davidson 1962; Ratford's Café, Danny Lyon.

Document B

Some examples of Jim Crow laws in the southern states of the US.

Buses All passenger stations in this state operated by any motor transportation company shall have separate waiting rooms or space and separate ticket windows for the white and coloured races. *Alabama*

Buses Every person operating a bus line in the city shall provide equal but separate accommodation for white people and negroes on his buses, by requiring the employees in charge thereof to assign passengers to seats on the vehicles under their charge in such manner as to separate the white people from the negroes, where there are both white and negroes in the same car... *Montgomery*

Restaurants It shall be unlawful to conduct a restaurant or other place for the serving of food in the city, at which white and coloured people are served in the same room, unless such white and coloured persons are effectually separated by a solid partition extending from the floor upward to a distance of seven feet or higher, and unless a separate entrance from the street is provided for each compartment. *Alabama*

Education Separate schools shall be maintained for the children of the white and coloured races. *Mississippi*

Source: www.spartacus.schoolnet.co.uk

1. (a) What is the main difference between the two photographs in Document A?
   (b) In Ratford's Café, how do the 'White' and 'Colored' entrances differ?
   (c) How were whites and coloured people segregated in bus passenger stations in Alabama, according to Document B?
   (d) What power had bus drivers in Montgomery, according to Document B?
   (e) How were whites and coloured people to be separated in a restaurant in Alabama, according to Document B?

2. (a) Which of the photographs in Document A is supported by the information in Document B?
   (b) Which of the Documents, A or B, gives a clearer understanding of Jim Crow laws? Explain your answer.

3. (a) What are the main differences between photographs, such as Document A, and written sources, such as Document B, as sources for historians?

(b) Are the photographs in Document A biased?

4. What factors in post-war America helped black Americans fight a successful campaign to change Jim Crow laws?

SAMPLE QUESTION 2

Document A

An account by Rosa Parks of the evening she refused to give up her seat in a Montgomery bus to white passengers.

...I left work on my way home December 1st, 1955. About six o'clock in the afternoon, I boarded the bus in downtown Montgomery on Court Square. As the bus proceeded out of town, on the third stop, the white passengers had filled the front of the bus. When I got on the bus the rear was filled with coloured passengers, and they were beginning to stand. The seat I occupied was the first of the seats where Negro passengers take on this route. The driver noted that the front of the bus was filled with white passengers, and there would be two or three men standing. He looked back and asked that the seats I had taken along with three other persons, one in the seat with me, and two across the aisle were seated. He demanded the seats we were occupying. The other passengers very reluctantly gave up their seats, but I refused to do so. He then called the officers of the law. They came and placed me under arrest, and I was bond, bailed out shortly after the arrest. And the trial was held December 5th on the next Monday, and the protest began from that date. And it is still continuin'.

Source: Extract from radio interview by Sidney Rogers, April 1956, quoted in Stewart Burns (ed.), *Daybreak of Freedom, The Montgomery Bus Boycott*, University of North Carolina Press, Chapel Hill, 1997, pp. 82–83.

Document B

A newspaper report from the Montgomery Advertiser, 5 December 1955 of the court case involving Rosa Parks.

Negress draws fine
Segregation case involving bus ride

By Bunny Honicker

A Negro woman was fined $10 and costs in police court here today for violation of a state law requiring racial segregation on city buses.

Rosa Parks, 634 Cleveland Ave., a seamstress at a downtown store, did not testify.

Negro Attorney (lawyer), Fred D. Gray informed Recorder's Court Judge John B. Scott he would appeal the decision to Montgomery Circuit Court. A few minutes later, Gray signed a $100 appeal bond for his client.

Also signing the woman's appeal bond was E. D. Nixon of Montgomery, a former state president of the National Association for the Advancement of Colored People.

Gray had entered a plea of innocent for his client, who stood silent throughout the hearing.

City Prosecutor Eugene Loe called Montgomery City Lines bus driver J. F. Blake to the stand to open the city's case. Blake briefly told how Rosa Parks refused to move to the rear of this bus last Thursday night after he had requested her and several others to move to make room for white passengers he was taking on near the Empire Theatre.

Blake said there were 22 Negroes and 14 whites seated in the 36-seat bus and that he asked several of the Negroes to move to the rear in order to equalise the seating.

Source: *The Montgomery Advertiser*, 5 December 1955.

1. (a) According to Document A, when did the incident involving Rosa Parks take place?
   (b) Where did Rosa Parks sit in the bus?
   (c) Who asked her to leave her seat, according to Documents A and B?
   (d) Why was Rosa Parks fined $10, according to Document B?
   (e) Who signed Rosa Parks's appeal bond, according to Document B?

2. (a) What information on Rosa Parks does Document B give us which Document A does not?

   (b) Does J.F. Blake's account (Document B) of what happened agree with Rosa Parks's (Document A)?

3. (a) What are the strengths and weaknesses of Document A as an historical source?

   (b) Is Document B more factual than Document A? Explain your answer.

4. Why did Rosa Parks's refusal to give up her seat lead to the Montgomery Bus Boycott?

SAMPLE QUESTION 3

Document A

Inez Jessie Baskin was assistant editor of the black edition of The Montgomery Advertiser *at the time of the Montgomery Bus Boycott.*

> About six o'clock one evening, I received a phone call from a friend's mother telling me to go to the Dexter Avenue Church. That's where I heard about Rosa Parks's arrest. I had first met Rosa Parks during the time that I was a member of the National Association for the Advancement of Colored People (NAACP). She had always impressed me. She was just an angel walking. When things happened that would upset most people, she would just give you this angelic smile, and that was the end of it.

Source: Inez Jessie Baskin, quoted in Peter Jennings and Todd Brewster, *The Century*, Doubleday, New York, 1998, p. 350.

Document B

E.D. Nixon was president of the local branch of the National Association for the Advancement of Colored People (NAACP).

> Montgomery's black establishment leaders decided they would have to wait for the right person. And that person, it transpired, would be Rosa Parks. 'Mrs Parks was a married woman,' said E.D. Nixon. 'She was morally clean, and she had a fairly good academic training... If there was ever a person we would've been able to (use to) break the situation that existed in the Montgomery city line, Rosa L. Parks was the woman to use... I probably would've examined a dozen (cases) before I got there if Rosa Parks hadn't come along before I found the right one.'

Source: E.D. Nixon, quoted by Gary Younge, 'She would not be moved', in *The Guardian*, 16 December 2000.

1. (a) Where did Inez Baskin first meet Rosa Parks, according to Document A?

   (b) Why did Rosa Parks always impress Inez Baskin?

   (c) Why did E.D. Nixon choose the Rosa Parks case, according to Document B?

   (d) How many cases did E.D. Nixon expect to examine if Rosa Parks had not come along?

   (e) What does he mean when he says, 'If there was ever a person we would've been able to (use to) break the situation that existed in the Montgomery city line, Rosa L. Parks was the woman to use'?

2. (a) What information does Document B give about Rosa Parks which is not given in Document A?

   (b) To what extent would you agree that Document A and Document B look at Rosa Parks from different points of view (perspectives)?

3. (a) Are both documents primary sources?

   (b) Document B is a newspaper account written long after the Montgomery Bus Boycott. How would that affect its usefulness and reliability as an historical source?

4. What did the Montgomery Bus Boycott contribute to the progress of the civil rights movement in the US?

SAMPLE QUESTION 4

Document A

Martin Luther King speaking at a mass meeting at Holt Street Baptist Church, Montgomery, 5 December 1955, the night Rosa Parks had been fined $10 for refusing to leave her seat on a Montgomery bus for a white passenger.

And you know my friends, there comes a time when people get tired of being trampled over by the iron feet of oppression... I want to say that we are not here advocating violence. We have never done that... We are a Christian people. We believe in the Christian religion. We believe in the teachings of Jesus. The only weapon that we have in our hands this evening is the weapon of protest. And certainly, certainly, this is the glory of America, with all its faults. This is the glory of our democracy. If we were incarcerated behind the iron curtain of a Communistic nation we couldn't do this... But the glory of American democracy is the right to protest for right... We are not wrong in what we are doing. If we are wrong, the Supreme Court of this nation is wrong. If we are wrong, God almighty is wrong.

Source: Transcript of audio recording of Martin Luther King's speech.

Document B

This account of the leadership of Martin Luther King is taken from the local paper, the Montgomery Advertiser, *just over one month after Rosa Parks's arrest.*

> There seems uncertainty in the minds of the white community of Montgomery over the identity of the director of the bus boycott. Who is the acknowledged leader? He seems to be Rev. Martin Luther King Jr., a 27-year-old Negro Baptist preacher. Rev. King does not speculate on the ultimate fruits of the Negro movement, but he does declare the current boycott is directed solely toward obtaining a better seating arrangement for Negro passengers. However, he is frank to admit that his own views are more ambitious. 'Frankly,' he says, 'I am for immediate integration. Segregation is evil, and I cannot, as a minister, condone evil.' ... King is a member of the Montgomery Improvement Association, a Negro organization of some 50 members which has been active in the conduct of the boycott. ... At all meetings where the boycott has been discussed, he is the one who has enunciated the Negro demands for better seating, more courtesy and the hiring of Negro drivers on predominantly Negro routes.

Source: Tom Johnson, 'The Rev. King is Boycott Boss', *Montgomery Advertiser*, 19 January 1956.

1. (a) What do the people get tired of, according to Martin Luther King in Document A?
   (b) If they were in a Communist country, what could they not do, according to Document A?
   (c) In Document B, what is the white community uncertain of?
   (d) According to Document B, what are the Negro demands?
   (e) In what way are Martin Luther King's views more ambitious?
2. (a) Which account – Document A or B – is more factual? Explain your answer.
   (b) Which document gives a better account of the views of Martin Luther King?
3. (a) What are the strengths and weaknesses of Document A as an historical source?
   (b) How useful and reliable is Document B as an historical source?
4. How significant a role did Martin Luther King play in the civil rights movement?

SAMPLE QUESTION 5

Document A

An extract from a history book describing a meeting of black ministers in Montgomery at the beginning of the bus boycott. Nixon was the local president of the National Association for the Advancement of Colored People (NAACP).

That evening (5 December, the day Rosa Parks was fined), Nixon assembled fifty ministers – the most influential leaders in the black community – to decide what to do next. Their response was disillusioning. Several ministers suggested timidly that one day (boycott) had been enough. Another group endorsed a longer boycott if their identities could be concealed. A boiling mad Nixon reproached the clerics: 'What the hell you people talkin' about? How you gonna to have a mass meeting, gonna boycott a city bus line without the white folks knowing it? … You oughta make up your mind right now that you goin' either admit you are a grown man or concede the fact that you are a bunch of scared boys.' Nixon's words splashed the preachers like a cold shower, and when the NAACP (National Association for the Advancement of Colored People) hesitated to get involved, they formed a new organisation called the Montgomery Improvement Association…

Source: From Bruce J. Dierenfield, *The Civil Rights Movement*, Seminar Studies in History, Pearson Education, England, 2004, p. 44. Professor Dierenfield is Professor of American History in Canisius College, Buffalo, New York.

Document B

Extracts describing the role of the churches and music in the Montgomery Bus Boycott.

The Montgomery Improvement Association organised the bus boycott in that Alabama town. Citizens involved in the boycott would gather in churches to share information, gather strength, hear from the movement's leaders, and raise their voices together in song. Martin Luther King's wife, Coretta, remembered that songs were always part of the Association's meetings. 'Someone would come and sing, without an instrument at all. Then they would have someone who played the piano or the organ, and they would start, just like they start at the church services. And they would sing the songs and the hymns of the church.' … One is 'Onward Christian Soldiers' – that song you would have heard mostly as a Sunday school song. If you wonder why that song could capture the power of what they were doing, look at the text:

Onward, Christian soldiers
Marching as to war
With the cross of Jesus
Going on before...

It is a battle song.

Source: From *Eyes on the Prize, America's Civil Rights Movement, 1954–85*, Public Broadcasting Service, at www.pbs.org/wgbh/amex/eyesontheprize/story/02_bus.html, and Bernice Johnson Reagon, *Music in the Civil Rights Movement*, at www.pbs.org/wgbh/amex/eyesontheprize/reflect/r03_music.html.

1. (a) Who were the most influential leaders of the black community, according to Document A?
   (b) What was the response of the black ministers at the beginning of the meeting organised by Nixon (Document A)?
   (c) Why did the citizens of Montgomery gather in churches, according to Document B?
   (d) What types of songs and hymns were sung, according to Coretta King?
   (e) Where would you hear 'Onward Christian Soldiers', according to Document B?
2. (a) From the information given in Document B, would you say E.D. Nixon was right to persuade black ministers to form the Montgomery Improvement Association (Document A)?
   (b) What are the differences in the meeting described in Document A and the church meetings of Document B?
3. (a) Are Documents A and B primary or secondary sources? Explain your answer.
   (b) Which document has more opinions or interpretations? Explain your answer.
4. What factors account for the success of black Americans in achieving civil rights in the US?

OTHER CONTEXTUAL QUESTIONS ON THE MONTGOMERY BUS BOYCOTT, 1955–56

1. What were the origins of the civil rights movement in the US?
2. What caused the Montgomery Bus Boycott?
3. How successful was Martin Luther King in improving the position of black Americans in US society?
4. Why was the Montgomery Bus Boycott (1956) so important in the story of the civil rights movement?
5. What part did the civil rights movement play in improving the position of black Americans in US society?
6. How successful was the civil rights movement in the US during the period 1945–68?
7. During the period 1945–89, what was the impact of racial conflict on US society?
8. What was the impact of the Montgomery Bus Boycott on the demand for civil rights in the US?
9. What tactics and methods were used by black Americans to win civil rights?
10. Why was there continued racial conflict in the US in the 1960s and 1970s in spite of the passage of civil rights laws?

THE US AND VIETNAM – TIMELINE

19th century	Indochina (Laos, Cambodia and Vietnam) taken over by French.
1941	(Second World War) Japanese invasion of Indochina; Ho Chi Minh and Vietminh fight them. Post-war Ho Chi Minh and Vietminh fight French; Truman supported French.
1949	Communist victory in China.
1950–53	Korean War.
1954	President Eisenhower sent US military advisers to help French and later South Vietnam. Fall of Dien Bien Phu; Geneva Accords – French withdraw; Indochina divided into Laos, Cambodia and North and South Vietnam.
1960	1,500 US advisers in South Vietnam.
1961–63	President Kennedy increased US advisers to 23,000; sent in Green Berets to help South Vietnamese Army against Vietminh and Viet Cong. (November) President Diem of South Vietnam assassinated. President Kennedy assassinated; Johnson became President.
August 1964	Gulf of Tonkin Incident; Tonkin Resolution. Johnson re-elected President.
1965	Operation Rolling Thunder – air bombardment of North Vietnam. US Marines land at Da Nang (South Vietnam) – first US combat troops.
1965–67	Growth of US forces to over half a million.
January 1968	Tet Offensive in South Vietnam.
May 1968	My Lai Massacre.
1986	Johnson ordered partial halt to bombing of North Vietnam; proposed peace talks; announced he would not seek re-election. Paris peace talks began.
1969	Nixon became President of US. March against Death – 300,000 in anti-war march past the White House.
1970	Nixon ordered invasion of Cambodia. Four students killed in Kent State University.
1972	Nixon visited China.
1973	Paris Peace Agreement. US withdrawal from South Vietnam.
1975	Fall of Saigon; North took over South – unification under Communist control.

Case Study: Lyndon Johnson and Vietnam, 1963–68

SAMPLE QUESTION 1

Document A

Edited extract from a speech by President Johnson at a news conference in the White House, 5 August 1965.

Three times in my lifetime – in two world wars and in Korea – Americans have gone to far lands to fight for freedom. We have learned at a terrible and brutal cost that retreat does not bring safety, and weakness does not bring peace. And it is this lesson that has brought us to Viet Nam. There are great stakes in the balance. Most of the nations of Asia cannot by themselves and alone resist the growing might and grasping ambition of Asian Communism. Our power, therefore, is a very vital shield. An Asia so threatened by Communist domination would imperil the security of the US itself. Moreover, we are in Vietnam to fulfil one of the most solemn pledges of the American nation. Three Presidents over 11 years have promised to defend this small and valiant nation. We cannot now dishonor our word.

Source: Quoted in *The Press Conference*, www.time.com.

Document B

The Blind Leading the Blind

Source: Cartoon drawn by David Levine, *The New York Times Review of Books*, 1971.

1. (a) According to President Johnson in Document A, why is 'our power' 'a vital shield'?
   (b) According to Document A, why is the security of the US in danger?
   (c) According to Document A, why is America in Vietnam?
   (d) What is the message of the cartoon in Document B?
   (e) Name and identify one of the presidents in the cartoon in Document B.
2. (a) Document A mentions three presidents, Document B pictures four presidents. Can you explain the difference?
   (b) Does President Johnson in Document A take the same view about US involvement in Vietnam as the cartoon in Document B?
3. (a) Document A is a public speech. How useful are public speeches as sources for historians?
   (b) Would you consider Document B biased? Explain your answer.
4. How did the US become involved in Vietnam?

SAMPLE QUESTION 2

Document A

Edited extract from President Johnson's television address, 4 August 1964, after the Tonkin Gulf Incident.

My fellow Americans:

As President and Commander in Chief, it is my duty to the American people to report that renewed hostile actions against US ships on the high seas in the Gulf of Tonkin have today required me to order the military forces of the United States to take action in reply.

The initial attack on the destroyer *Maddox*, on August 2, was repeated today by a number of hostile vessels attacking two US destroyers with torpedoes. The destroyers, and supporting aircraft, acted at once on the orders I gave after the initial act of aggression.

We believe at least two of the attacking boats were sunk. There were no US losses...

I shall immediately request the Congress to pass a resolution making it clear that our Government is united in its determination to take all necessary measures in support of freedom, and in defence of peace, in South-East Asia.

Source: Australian Associated Press – Reuters News Agency, quoted in *The Age*, 6 August 1964.

Document B

Extract from an historian's view of the Memo by Robert McNamara, Secretary of Defence, to President Johnson, 20 July 1965.

With the situation (in Vietnam) continuing to deteriorate (in 1965), McNamara wrote a decisive memo in late July. It laid out three options: 'cut our losses and withdraw', 'continue at about the same level' or 'expand promptly and substantially the US pressure'. McNamara urged rejection of the first option as 'humiliating the United States and very damaging to our future effectiveness on the world scene.' The second option would 'confront us later with a choice between withdrawal and emergency expansion of forces, perhaps too late to do any good.' He recommended the third. It would lead to 'considerable cost in casualties and material' but would 'offer a good chance of producing a favourable settlement in the long run.'

Source: Quoted in James T. Patterson, *Grand Expectations, The United States, 1945–74*, Oxford University Press, Oxford, 1996.

1. (a) What ship was attacked on 2 August, according to Document A?
   (b) How were the ships attacked on 4 August, according to the document?
   (c) Which side was more successful on 4 August?
   (d) What was one of the options, according to McNamara in Document B?
   (e) Why did McNamara select one of the options?
2. (a) What is the difference in the style of language of the two documents, A and B? Explain your answer.
   (b) Do both documents favour aggression against the North Vietnamese and Vietcong?
3. (a) What evidence is there in Document A to show it is biased?
   (b) Document B is a secondary source which is using edited extracts of a primary source. What problems does that present in assessing Document B as a source for historians?
4. To what extent was the Tonkin Gulf Incident a turning point in US policy in relation to Vietnam?

SAMPLE QUESTION 3

Document A

Extract from President Johnson's message to Congress, 4 August 1964, after the Tonkin Gulf Incident.

Our policy in southeast Asia has been consistent and unchanged since 1954. I summarized it on June 2 in four simple propositions:

1. America keeps her word. Here as elsewhere, we must and shall honor our commitments.

2. The issue is the future of southeast Asia as a whole. A threat to any nation in that region is a threat to all, and a threat to us.

3. Our purpose is peace. We have no military, political, or territorial ambitions in the area.

4. This is not just a jungle war, but a struggle for freedom on every front of human activity. Our military and economic assistance to South Vietnam and Laos in particular has the purpose of helping these countries to repel aggression and strengthen their independence.

The threat to the free nations of southeast Asia has long been clear. The North Vietnamese regime has constantly sought to take over South Vietnam and Laos.

Source: The American Presidency Project, www.presidency.ucsb.edu.

Document B

Extract from the US State Department White Paper* on Vietnam, 27 February 1965, explaining US involvement in Vietnam.

South Vietnam is fighting for its life against a brutal campaign of terror and armed attack inspired, directed, supplied, and controlled by the Communist regime in Hanoi...in Vietnam a totally new brand of aggression has been loosed against an independent people who want to make their way in peace and freedom. ... North Vietnam's commitment to seize control of the South is no less total than was the commitment of the regime in North Korea in 1950. ... In recent months new types of weapons have been introduced in the VC (Vietcong) army, for which all ammunition must come from outside sources. Communist China and other Communist states have been the prime suppliers of these weapons and ammunition. ... The people of South Vietnam have chosen to resist this threat. At their request, the United States has taken its place beside them in their defensive struggle.

* White Papers are issued by governments. They lay out policy or proposed action on a topic of current concern.

Source: US Department of State Bulletin, Vol. 52, No. 1343, March 1965, pp. 404–27.

1. (a) According to Document A, what is the purpose of US policy in south-east Asia?
    (b) What countries in south-east Asia are threatened by aggression?
    (c) Who is organising the campaign against South Vietnam, according to Document B?
    (d) What is the attack against South Vietnam compared to?
    (e) Where are the new weapons for the Vietcong coming from, according to Document B?
2. (a) Do Documents A and B agree on the causes of the conflict in Vietnam? Explain your answer.
    (b) What do the documents say about the role of the US?
3. (a) Are both documents biased? Explain your answer.
    (b) Do you agree that Document A is better at presenting its case?
4. To what extent did the political and military policies of President Johnson lead to greater US involvement in Vietnam?

SAMPLE QUESTION 4

Document A

Photograph from an anti-war demonstration in New York, 1967.

Source: Eli Finer, photographer.

"There's Money Enough To Support Both Of You —
Now, Doesn't That Make You Feel Better?"

---from The Herblock Gallery (Simon & Schuster, 1968)

Document B

*Johnson is represented as
Administration in the centre.*

'There's money enough to support
both of you…Now, doesn't that
make you feel better?' - A 1967
Herblock Cartoon, copyright by
The Herb Block Foundation.
Washington Post.

Document C

'*The Train Robbery' – Johnson
is shown with an axe breaking
up the Great Society.*

Source: A cartoon from *Punch*
magazine, published in Britain
in 1967.

1. (a) According to Document A, what is the monetary and the educational cost of one air-to-air missile programme?
   (b) What does the cost of six schools equal?
   (c) Describe how the women in Document B are dressed.
   (d) What is the message of the Administration in Document B?
   (e) What is keeping 'Vietnam' and the 'Great Society' going, according to Document C?
2. (a) What information in Document A relates to 'US Urban Needs' in Document B?
   (b) Do Documents A, B and C agree or disagree? Explain your answer.
3. (a) Are Documents A and B primary or secondary sources? Explain your answer.
   (b) Are Documents A and C propaganda? Explain your answer.
4. What was the impact of the Vietnam War on Johnson's presidency?

SAMPLE QUESTION 5

Document A

Edited extract from an article by US Secretary of Defence, Clark Clifford, on the impact of the Tet Offensive, 1968. Clark Clifford was appointed Secretary of Defence in 1968 after Robert McNamara and he served until the end of the Johnson presidency (January 1969).

When I asked for a presentation of the military plan for attaining victory in Viet Nam, I was told that there was no plan for victory in the historic American sense. Why not? Because our forces were operating under three major political restrictions [limitations]: The President had forbidden the invasion of North Viet Nam because this could trigger the mutual assistance pact between North Viet Nam and China; the President had forbidden the mining of the harbour at Haiphong, the principal port through which the North received military supplies, because a Soviet vessel might be sunk; the President had forbidden our forces to pursue the enemy into Laos and Cambodia, for to do so would spread the war. ... 'Given these circumstances, how can we win?' We would, I was told, continue to evidence our superiority over the enemy; we would continue to attack in the belief that he would reach the stage where he would find it inadvisable to go on with the war. He could not afford the attrition we were inflicting on him. And we were improving our posture [position] all the time.

Source: Clark Clifford, 'A Viet Nam Reappraisal', in *Foreign Affairs*, July 1969, published by the Council on Foreign Relations, New York.

Document B

President Lyndon B. Johnson's Address to the Nation on 31 March 1968, announcing his decision not to seek re-election as President (and steps to limit the war in Vietnam).

For 37 years in the service of our Nation, first as a Congressman, as a Senator, and as Vice President, and now as your President, I have put the unity of the people first. ... There is division in the American house now. There is divisiveness among us all tonight. And holding the trust that is mine, as President of all the people, I cannot disregard the peril [danger] to the progress of the American people and the hope and the prospect of peace for all peoples... What we won when all of our people united must not now be lost in suspicion, distrust, selfishness, and politics among any of our people.

Believing this as I do, I have concluded that I should not permit the Presidency to become involved in the partisan divisions that are developing in this political year. ... I do not believe that I should devote an hour or a day of my time to any personal partisan causes or to any duties other than the awesome duties of this office – the Presidency of your country.

Accordingly, I shall not seek, and I will not accept, the nomination of my party for another term as your President.

Source: *Public Papers of the Presidents of the United States: Lyndon B. Johnson, 1968–69.* Volume I, Government Printing Office, Washington, DC, 1970, pp. 469–76.

1. (a) According to Document A, what military plan existed for attaining victory in the Vietnam War?
   (b) Why did the President forbid the invasion of North Vietnam?
   (c) How was the US going to win, according to Document A?
   (d) In Document B, what is the peril to the progress of the American people?
   (e) What is meant by 'this political year'?
2. (a) How does the main concern of Clark Clifford in Document A differ from the main concern of President Johnson in Document B?
   (b) Which document is better at helping you understand why America lost in Vietnam?
3. (a) Do you agree that Documents A and B are primary sources? Explain your answer.
   (b) What are the strengths and weaknesses as a historical source of an article such as Clark Clifford's in *Foreign Affairs*?

4. Why did the US withdraw from Vietnam?

OTHER CONTEXTUAL QUESTIONS ON JOHNSON AND VIETNAM

1. How successful was President Johnson in dealing with Vietnam during his presidency?
2. What policies did President Johnson follow in relation to the war in Vietnam?
3. What factors influenced Johnson's policy on Vietnam?
4. What factors influenced US policy on Vietnam?
5. Which had the greater impact on the US – involvement in Korea or involvement in Vietnam? Argue your case, referring to both.
6. What were the main developments in US foreign policy in the 1960s?
7. To what extent was the Vietnam War a 'personal tragedy' for Johnson and a 'national tragedy' for the US?
8. To what extent were the Tonkin Gulf Incident and the Tet Offensive turning points in US involvement in Vietnam?
9. To what extent did domestic factors influence US policy in Vietnam?
10. Why did the US become involved in armed conflict in Vietnam and why did it eventually withdraw from that country?
11. What was the impact of the Vietnam War on the US?
12. What was the impact of the Vietnam War on the US economy and society?
13. To what extent did the Vietnam War contribute to the divisions in US society in the late 1960s and early 1970s?

SPACE EXPLORATION AND THE MOON LANDING – TIMELINE

1939–45   (Second World War) German scientists, including Werner Von Braun, develop V1 (flying bombs) and V2 (rockets) to bomb Britain.

1945   Von Braun and other German scientists surrendered to American troops; US captured V2 rockets and took them to US.

1950s   Development of ICBMs (inter-continental ballistic missiles) to carry nuclear bombs in the Cold War.

1957   Russians launch first space rocket – the *Sputnik*. US *Vanguard* exploded on the launch pad.

1958   Launch of first ICBM – the Atlas; later use of Titan and Minuteman rockets with longer range.

1958   First US rocket, *Explorer 1*, launched successfully. NASA (National Aeronautics and Space Administration) set up to organise US space exploration.

1960   Launch of first US weather satellite.

1961   Russians sent first man into space – Yuri Gagarin. Mercury Project: Alan Shepard, first American astronaut in space, in *Freedom 7*. President Kennedy's speech promising that America would have a man on the moon 'before the decade is out'.

1962   *Friendship 7* with John Glenn orbited Earth three times. *Telstar*, US communications satellite, beamed first live transatlantic telecast.

1965   Gemini programme: first flights sending two astronauts into space. Space walks and space rendezvous part of programme.

1968   Apollo mission: first manned *Apollo* missions sending three astronauts into space. *Apollo 8* made manned orbit of the moon and sent back television pictures.

1969   Moon landing: *Apollo 11* took Neil Armstrong, Buzz Aldrin and Michael Collins to the moon; Armstrong and Aldrin used the moon module, *Eagle*, to land on the moon. *Apollo 12* collected soil samples from moon.

1970s   Launch of unmanned space probes to planets such as Jupiter, Mars, Mercury and Venus to find signs of life.

1970   *Apollo 13* cancelled moon landing due to technical difficulties and returned to Earth.

1971	*Apollo 14* landed on the moon and carried out scientific experiments. *Apollo 15* used a moon buggy to get around the moon surface.
1972	*Apollo 16* and *17* landed on the moon; *Apollo 17* was the last manned flight to the moon up to the present.
1973	*Skylab* launched, US manned space exploration station.
1976	*Viking 2*, an unmanned rocket, landed on Mars.
1980s	Development of space shuttle.
1981	*Columbia*, first successful flight by space shuttle.
1986	Explosion of space shuttle *Challenger* stopped use of space shuttles for three years.

Case Study: The Moon Landing, 1969

SAMPLE QUESTION 1

Document A

President John F. Kennedy speaking before a joint session of Congress on Urgent National Needs, 25 May 1961.

If we are to win the battle that is now going on around the world between freedom and tyranny, the dramatic achievements in space which occurred in recent weeks should have made clear to us all, as did the *Sputnik* in 1957, the impact of this adventure on the minds of men everywhere, who are attempting to make a determination of which road they should take... I believe that this nation should commit itself to achieving the goal, before this decade is out, of landing a man on the moon and returning him safely to the earth. No single space project in this period will be more impressive to mankind, or more important for the long-range exploration of space; and none will be so difficult or expensive to accomplish. ... An additional 23 million dollars, together with 7 million dollars already available, will accelerate development of the *Rover* nuclear rocket. ... An additional 50 million dollars will make the most of our present leadership, by accelerating the use of space satellites for world-wide communications... An additional 75 million dollars will help give us at the earliest possible time a satellite system for world-wide weather observation.

Source: Special Message to the Congress on Urgent National Needs, 25 May 1961, John F. Kennedy Presidential Library and Museum, Historical Sources, www.jfklibrary.org.

Document B

President Kennedy's Address at Rice University, Houston, Texas on the Nation's Space Effort, 12 September 1962.

There is no strife, no prejudice, no national conflict in outer space as yet. Its hazards are hostile to us all. Its conquest deserves the best of all mankind, and its opportunity for peaceful cooperation may never come again. But why, some say, the moon? Why choose this as our goal? And they may well ask why climb the highest mountain? Why, 35 years ago, fly the Atlantic? … We choose to go to the moon in this decade and do the other things, not because they are easy, but because they are hard, because that goal will serve to organize and measure the best of our energies and skills, because that challenge is one that we are willing to accept, one we are unwilling to postpone, and one which we intend to win, and the others, too. … Within these last 19 months at least 45 satellites have circled the earth. Some 40 of them were 'made in the United States of America' and they were far more sophisticated and supplied far more knowledge to the people of the world than those of the Soviet Union… Transit satellites are helping our ships at sea to steer a safer course. Tiros satellites have given us unprecedented warnings of hurricanes and storms, and will do the same for forest fires and icebergs… And finally, the space effort itself, while still in its infancy, has already created a great number of new companies, and tens of thousands of new jobs.

Source: Address at Rice University on the Nation's Space Effort, 12 September 1962, John F. Kennedy Presidential Library and Museum, Historical Sources, www.jfklibrary.org.

1. (a) According to President Kennedy in Document A, what battle is now going on around the world?
   (b) To what goal does he say the nation should commit itself?
   (c) What is the additional money being spent on in Document A?
   (d) In Document B, what reasons does President Kennedy give for choosing the moon as a goal?
   (e) How many satellites in the previous 19 months were American, according to Document B?
2. (a) What reason(s) does President Kennedy give for space exploration in Document A which he does not give in Document B?
   (b) Which document is more persuasive in making the case for space exploration?

3. (a) How useful and reliable are public speeches as sources for historians of the moon landing?

   (b) What evidence is there in the documents that President Kennedy is trying to convince his audiences that space exploration is worthwhile?

4. Why did the US plan a moon landing during the 1960s?

SAMPLE QUESTION 2

Document A

This is a news report from the Irish Independent, *21 July 1969.*

Man sets foot on the moon for the first time

US astronaut Neil Armstrong, commander of moonship *Eagle*, at 4.00 a.m. this morning (Irish time) was the first man to walk on the moon's crusted surface. Armstrong's first words were, 'That's one small step for man, one giant leap for mankind.' He began a description of his own footprints 'in the small sandy particles' under his feet. 'There seems to be no difficulty moving around.' Earlier, Neil Armstrong and his companion, Edwin Aldrin, had landed safely on the moon in the *Eagle* module. It was a landing which nearly ended in disaster, for, as the module neared the moon's surface, Armstrong saw that the computerised, automatic pilot was sending the fragile ship towards a field scattered with rocks in the projected landing site on the moon's Sea of Tranquillity. He grabbed control of his ship, sent it clear of the area where it would have met almost certain disaster, and landed four miles beyond the original landing point. It was a costly manoeuvre. It cut the available fuel short. When it landed, *Eagle* had barely 49 seconds of rocket fuel left.

Source: *Irish Independent*, 21 July 1969, reproduced from *Irish Independent, 100 Years in the News, 1905–2005*, Dublin.

Document B

An historian's account of the moon landing.

The Eagle Has Landed

Now Armstrong saw that the place he had selected was no good. 'I'm going right over a crater,' he said [to Aldrin], 'I gotta get farther over there.' Again he nudged the hand controller forward, levelling the aircraft, using the last bit of forward speed to clear the crater. And just beyond it he saw where he was going to land. It was a smooth, level place about 200 feet square, bounded on one side by a few large craters and on the other by a line of boulders... Armstrong clicked the rate-of-descent toggle until *Eagle* descended no faster than an elevator... Fifty feet above the moon. Now thirty... With the engine still firing, *Eagle* settled onto the moon so gently that neither man sensed the contact. Quickly Armstrong hit the ENGINE STOP button and said, 'Shutdown.' ... Then there was a moment of quiet, and the two men turned to one another in the tiny cabin. Their eyes met, their bearded faces grinned at each other inside bubble helmets, and their gloved hands clasped. Armstrong keyed his microphone. 'Houston, Tranquillity Base here. The *Eagle* has landed.'

Source: Andrew Chaikin, *A Man on the Moon, The Voyages of the Apollo Astronauts*, Michael Joseph, London, 1994, pp. 198–200.

1. (a) In Document A, how did Armstrong describe the surface of the moon?
   (b) Why did the landing nearly end in disaster, according to Document A?
   (c) How far away from the original landing point did Armstrong eventually land?
   (d) In Document B, where did Armstrong see he was going to land?
   (e) What was the reaction of both men to the landing, according to Document B?
2. (a) How does different information in each account give you a better understanding of what happened when the *Eagle* was landed?
   (b) Which account, A or B, gives a better description of the difficulty in landing the *Eagle*?
3. (a) Are both of the documents secondary accounts of the landing? Explain your answer.
   (b) Which document do you think is more reliable?
4. How did advances in technology contribute to the moon landing in 1969?

SAMPLE QUESTION 3

Document A

LATE CITY EDITION
Weather: Rain, warm today; clear tonight. Sunny, pleasant tomorrow. Temp. range: today 80-66; Sunday 71-66. Temp.-Hum. Index yesterday 69. Complete U.S. report on P. 50.

"All the News That's Fit to Print"

The New York Times

VOL. CXVIII..No. 40,721   NEW YORK, MONDAY, JULY 21, 1969   10 CENTS

MEN WALK ON MOON

ASTRONAUTS LAND ON PLAIN; COLLECT ROCKS, PLANT FLAG

Voice From Moon: 'Eagle Has Landed'

EAGLE (the lunar module): Houston, Tranquility Base here. The Eagle has landed.

HOUSTON: Roger, Tranquility, we copy you on the ground. You've got a bunch of guys about to turn blue. We're breathing again. Thanks a lot.

TRANQUILITY BASE: Thank you.

HOUSTON: You're looking good here.

TRANQUILITY BASE: A very smooth touchdown.

HOUSTON: Eagle, you are stay for T1. [The first step in the lunar operation.] Over.

TRANQUILITY BASE: Roger. Stay for T1.

HOUSTON: Roger and we see you venting 'the ox.

TRANQUILITY BASE: Roger.

COLUMBIA (the command and service module): How do you read us?

HOUSTON: Columbia, he has landed Tranquility Base. Eagle is at Tranquility. I read you five by. Over.

COLUMBIA: Yes, I heard the whole thing.

HOUSTON: Well, it's a good show.

COLUMBIA: Fantastic.

TRANQUILITY BASE: I'll second that.

APOLLO CONTROL: The next major stay-no stay will be for the T3 event. That is at 21 minutes 26 seconds after initiation of power descent.

COLUMBIA: Up telemetry command reset to reacquire on high gain.

HOUSTON: Copy. Out.

APOLLO CONTROL: We have an unofficial time for that touchdown of 102 hours, 45 minutes, 42 seconds and we will update that.

TRANQUILITY BASE: Eagle, you loaded R2 wrong. We want 10254.

HOUSTON: That's affirmative.

APOLLO CONTROL: We're now less than four minutes from our next stay-no stay. It will be for one complete revolution of the command module.

One of the first things that Armstrong and Aldrin will do after getting their next stay-no stay will be to remove their helmets and gloves.

HOUSTON: Eagle, you are stay for T2. Over.

Continued on Page 4, Col. 1

VOYAGE TO THE MOON

By Archibald MacLeish

Presence among us,

    wanderer in our skies,

dazzle of silver in our leaves and on our waters silver,

    O

silver evasion in our farthest thought—
"the visiting moon" . . . "the glimpses of the moon" . . .

and we have touched you!

    From the first of time,
before the first of time, before the
first men tasted time, we thought of you.
You were a wonder to us, unattainable,
a longing past the reach of longing,
a light beyond our light, our lives—perhaps
a meaning to us . . .

    Now
our hands have touched you in your depth of night.

Three days and three nights we journeyed,
steered by farthest stars, climbed outward,
crossed the invisible tide-rip where the floating dust
falls one way or the other in the void between,
followed that other down, encountered
cold, faced death—unfathomable emptiness . . .

Then, the fourth day evening, we descended,
made fast, set foot at dawn upon your beaches,
sifted between our fingers your cold sand.

We stand here in the dusk, the cold, the silence . . .

and here, as at the first of time, we lift our heads.
Over us, more beautiful than the moon, a
moon, a wonder to us, unattainable,
a longing past the reach of longing,
a light beyond our light, our lives—perhaps
a meaning to us . . .

    O, a meaning!

over us on these silent beaches the bright
earth,

    presence among us

Neil A. Armstrong moves away from the leg of the landing craft after taking the first step on the surface of the moon

Col. Edwin E. Aldrin Jr. climbing down the ladder. The television camera was attached to a side of the lunar module.

The New York Times from C.B.S. News

A Powdery Surface Is Closely Explored

By JOHN NOBLE WILFORD
Special to The New York Times

HOUSTON, Monday, July 21—Men have landed and walked on the moon.

Two Americans, astronauts of Apollo 11, steered their fragile four-legged lunar module safely and smoothly to the historic landing yesterday at 4:17:40 P.M., Eastern daylight time.

Neil A. Armstrong, the 38-year-old civilian commander, radioed to earth and the mission control room here:

"Houston, Tranquility Base here. The Eagle has landed."

The first men to reach the moon—Mr. Armstrong and his co-pilot, Col. Edwin E. Aldrin Jr. of the Air Force—brought their ship to rest on a level, rock-strewn plain near the southwestern shore of the arid Sea of Tranquility.

About six and a half hours later, Mr. Armstrong satisfied himself that the lunar soil was firm and set the landing craft's hatch, stepped slowly down the ladder and declared as he planted the first human footprint on the lunar crust:

"That's one small step for man, one giant leap for mankind."

His first step on the moon came at 10:56:20 P.M., as a television camera outside the craft transmitted his every move to an awed and excited audience of hundreds of millions of people on earth.

Tentative Steps Test Soil

Mr. Armstrong's initial steps were tentative tests of the lunar soil's firmness and of his ability to move about easily in his bulky white spacesuit and backpacks and under the influence of lunar gravity, which is one-sixth that of the earth.

"The surface is fine and powdery," the astronaut reported. "I can pick it up loosely with my toe. It does adhere in fine layers like powdered charcoal to the sole and sides of my boots. I only go in a small fraction of an inch, maybe an eighth of an inch. But I can see the footprints of my boots in the treads in the fine sandy particles."

After 19 minutes of Mr. Armstrong's testing, Colonel Aldrin joined him outside the craft.

The two men got busy setting up another television camera out from the lunar module, planting an American flag into the ground, scooping up soil and rock samples, deploying scientific experiments and hopping and loping about in a demonstration of their lunar agility.

They found walking and working on the moon less taxing than had been forecast. Mr. Armstrong once reported he was "very comfortable."

And people back on earth found the black-and-white television pictures of the bug-shaped lunar module and the men tramping about it so sharp and clear as to seem unreal, more like a toy and toy-like figures than human beings on the most daring and far-reaching expedition thus far undertaken.

Nixon Telephones Congratulations

During one break in the astronauts' work, President Nixon congratulated them from the White House in what, he said, "certainly has to be the most historic telephone call ever made."

"Because of what you have done," the President told the astronauts, "the heavens have become a part of man's world. And as you talk to us from the Sea of Tranquility, it requires us to redouble our efforts to bring peace and tranquility to earth.

"For one priceless moment in the whole history of man all the people on this earth are truly one—one in their pride in what you have done and one in our prayers that you will return safely to earth."

Mr. Armstrong replied:

"Thank you Mr. President. It's a great honor and privilege for us to be here representing not only the United States but men of peace of all nations, men with interests and a curiosity and men with a vision for the future."

Mr. Armstrong and Colonel Aldrin returned to their landing craft and closed the hatch at 1:12 A.M., 2 hours 21 minutes after opening the hatch on the moon. While the third member of the crew, Lieut. Col. Michael Collins of the Air Force, kept his orbital vigil overhead in the command ship, the two moon explorers settled down to sleep.

Outside their vehicle the astronauts had found a bleak

Continued on Page 2, Col. 1

Today's 4-Part Issue of The Times

This morning's issue of The New York Times is divided into four parts. The first part is devoted to news of Apollo 11, and including Editorials and letters to the Editor (Page 16). Poems on the landing on the moon appear on Page 17.

General news begins on the first page of the second part. The News Summary and Index is on the first page of the third part, which includes sports news, obituaries (Page 33) and transportation news and weather reports (Pages 50 and 51).

Financial and business news begins on the first page of the fourth part.

Following is the News Index for today's issue:

Mr. Armstrong, right, and Colonel Aldrin raise the U.S. flag. A metal rod at right angles to the mast keeps flag unfurled

Associated Press

Source: *The New York Times*, 21 July 1969.

Document B

THE IRISH TIMES

DUBLIN, MONDAY, JULY 21, 1969

PRICE 6d. (9d. in England)   No. 36,901   8.56 a.m. EDITION

TWO MEN WALK ON THE MOON

'One small step for man. One giant leap for mankind'

ARMSTRONG PILOTS EAGLE MANUALLY IN LAST STAGES OF LUNAR DESCENT

AT 20 SECONDS AFTER 3.56 A.M. (Irish time) today, the first man set foot on the Moon. He was Neil Armstrong, commander of the Apollo-11 mission, who, almost seven hours earlier—at 9.17 and 45 seconds—had piloted the lunar landing module, Eagle, to an almost perfect landing in the Sea of Tranquility.

At 4.14 he was joined on the surface of the Moon by his companion in the module, Edwin Aldrin.

Armstrong's first words on the Moon were : "That's one small step for man. One giant leap for mankind."

The hatch of the lunar module opened at 3.40. But before placing his foot on the top rung of the descent ladder Armstrong stood on the threshold and communicated his first impressions of lunar gravity and what he could see back to Earth.

A short way down the ladder, he said : "Okay, I'm going to pull it down." He referred to the instrument pack containing the television camera.

At the bottom, Armstrong said his foot sank into the surface very, very slightly, " but I can see my footprint." " There seems to be no difficulty in moving around," he said as he moved away from Eagle's leg.

The first earthmen on another planet—Neil Armstrong and Edwin Aldrin.

The two astronauts as they made their epic walk on the Moon this morning.

Pope: Do not forget war and hunger

POPE PAUL said yesterday that war and hunger around the world should not be forgotten in the race to conquer space.

'HEARTFELT' TRIBUTE FROM LOVELL
Paine's prediction

AFTER watching the Apollo touch-down, Sir Bernard Lovell, director of Jodrell Bank Observatory, said : "The moment of the landing was one of the moments of greatest drama in the history of man."

Luna-15 in orbit over Sea of Tranquillity

THE SOVIET Luna-15 craft last night swung into a new orbit bringing it only ten miles from the lunar surface.

FLAG ERECTED

FLAWLESS FLIGHT OF THE EAGLE
Armstrong picks safe site

APOLLO-11's journey into history began last Wednesday from Cape Kennedy. After an almost flawless three-day flight, the joined command ship and lunar module swept into an orbit of the Moon on Saturday afternoon.

Drowned in Kennedy car

Miss Mary Jo Kopechne (29), of Washington, who was drowned on Friday at Edgartown, Martha's an automobile driven by Senator Edward Kennedy.

COMMUNION BREAD IS TAKEN TO MOON

COLONEL EDWIN ALDRIN took to the Moon yesterday with a piece of Communion bread which he will use there to symbolise fellowship with the members of his home Church at Houston, Texas.

SAFE FROM SOLAR RADIATION

ARMSTRONG and Aldrin will be safe from harmful solar radiation.

Source: *The Irish Times*, 21 July 1969.

1. (a) What did the astronauts do, according to the headlines in Document A?

    (b) How does *The New York Times* describe the surface of the moon?

    (c) How did Armstrong pilot the *Eagle* on the last stages of lunar ascent, according to the headlines in *The Irish Times* (Document B)?

    (d) What was the message of the Pope, according to Document B?

    (e) What was taken to the moon, according to *The Irish Times*?

2. (a) What extra information is given in the headlines of *The Irish Times* which is not given in *The New York Times*?

    (b) What are the differences in the layout of the front pages?

3. (a) Is there bias shown in the layout and information of either front page?

    (b) What are the advantages and disadvantages of newspapers as sources for historians of the moon landing in 1969?

4. To what extent do you agree with the view that the success of the moon landing in 1969 was due as much to human skill as to technological development?

SAMPLE QUESTION 4

Document A

Astronaut Michael Collins's address to the Joint Meeting of the two Houses of Congress to receive the Apollo 11 *Astronauts, 16 September 1969.*

Colonel COLLINS. ... Many years before there was a space program my father had a favorite quotation: 'He who would bring back the wealth of the Indies must take the wealth of the Indies with him.' This we have done. We have taken to the moon the wealth of this Nation. ... We have brought back rocks. And I think it is a fair trade. ... May these rocks unlock the mystery of the origin of the moon, of our earth, and even of our solar system... We cannot ignore either the wealth of the Indies nor the realities of the immediate needs of our cities, our citizens, or our civics. We cannot launch our planetary probes [space explorations] from a springboard of poverty, discrimination, or unrest. But neither can we wait until each and every terrestrial problem has been solved. Such logic 200 years ago would have prevented expansion westward past the Appalachian Mountains [in America], for assuredly the eastern seaboard was beset by problems of great urgency then, as it is today. Man has always gone where he has been able to go. It is that simple. He will continue pushing back his frontier, no matter how far it may carry him from his homeland.

Source: Congressional Record – House of Representatives, Washington, DC, 16 September 1969.

Document B

1. (a) According to Collins in Document A, what did they take to the moon and what did they bring back?
   (b) What can't we wait for, according to Document A?
   (c) What motivates 'man', according to Collins in Document A?
   (d) Who are represented in Document B?
   (e) What is the message of Document B?

2. (a) What point does Collins make in Document A which contradicts the message of the cartoon in Document B?
   (b) Which document, A or B, is better at getting its point across?

3. (a) Is there evidence of bias in both documents?
   (b) Which are most useful and reliable as sources for historians – a public speech or a cartoon?

4. What was the impact of space exploration on America?

"Don't you feel comforted at the thought of all the benefits it'll bring to future generations?"

Source: A cartoon from *Punch* magazine, published in Britain in 1969.

OTHER CONTEXTUAL QUESTIONS ON THE MOON LANDING, 1969

1. What was the importance of the moon landing in 1969?
2. To what extent can the moon landing in 1969 be seen both as a major advance in technology and as a statement of American foreign policy?
3. What were the main advances in US space technology up to 1989?
4. What factors influenced the progress of US space exploration from 1945 to 1989?
5. To what extent was the moon landing in 1969 a turning point in US space exploration?
6. Was the moon landing a turning point in US space exploration?
7. To what extent were major advances made in US space technology between 1945 and 1989?
8. How significant were advances in US space technology up to 1989?
9. How and why did the US succeed in landing men on the moon in 1969?
10. What factors influenced the development of US space technology from 1945 to 1989?
11. How successful were advances in US space technology (or exploration) up to 1989?

Answering Question 2 (Comparison) and Question 3 (Criticism) in the Documents Study

In answering Q2 and Q3, you should make use of information from both documents (or all, if there are three documents).

We can use **Sample Question 1 from the Lyndon Johnson and Vietnam, 1963–68 Case Study** as an example.

Q2(a) asks, 'Document A mentions three presidents, Document B pictures four presidents. Can you explain the difference?'

In your answer, you could point to information in Document A such as 'over 11 years' from when Johnson spoke in 1965 – this would be 1954, so the three presidents he is referring to are Eisenhower, Kennedy and Johnson himself. But you can point out that the cartoon in Document B was drawn in 1971. By that time, Johnson had not gone forward for re-election and Nixon had been elected president. You can draw your conclusion from that.

Q2(b) asks, 'Does President Johnson in Document A take the same view about US involvement in Vietnam as the cartoon in Document B?'

In your answer, point out that Johnson does not take the same view as the cartoon. You can refer to words and phrases in the document such as 'to fight for freedom', 'vital shield', 'solemn pledges' and 'cannot dishonor' in support of the view that Johnson supports the war. But the cartoon treats all presidents the same, blindly leading the US into Vietnam – blindness here representing ignorance. You can also refer to Nixon diving in.

Q3(a) asks, 'Document A is a public speech. How useful are public speeches as sources for historians?'

In your answer, you should refer to evidence from the document as well as public speeches generally. This speech can give historians information as to why the US went to war. It will be accurate because it was recorded and transcribed. Speeches are used by politicians to give information to the public, their voters. But public speeches are also used to convince the public, so they are also propaganda. They may not give all the information. Therefore, public speeches may not give the politician's real thinking, and historians will need other sources to verify what is in the speech.

Q3(b) asks, 'Would you consider Document B biased?'

You can say yes or no here, but the main point is to support your answer with evidence from the document. In your answer, you can briefly explain 'bias'. Then you can refer to bias in the cartoon by saying the presidents are drawn in caricature. They are shown stumbling, blind and falling over. This is not showing respect for the presidents of the US – it is laughing at them, as they are made to look silly. It is also showing them as lacking in intelligence and independent thought. The artist is trying to say the presidents were responsible for leading the US into war. There is no effort made to explain the reasons the presidents may have had for going to war. But by 1971, many Americans were anti-war, so maybe the artist is reflecting majority opinion.

In summary, in answering Q2 and Q3 of the documents study, use evidence from both documents as well as evidence about the documents given in the caption(s) of the documents.

CASE STUDY: THE MONTGOMERY BUS BOYCOTT, 1955–56

The answers to Q4 (Contextualisation) in the documents–based Case Studies should be about two pages long.
You should use the essay plans which follow to practise writing paragraphs or full answers.

What factors in post-war America helped black Americans fight a successful campaign to change Jim Crow laws?

Intro: Blacks in post-war America – Jim Crow, discrimination, segregation in South – progress of CR movement, success by 1960s, end of Jim Crow, Supreme Court decisions, Civil Rights Act 1964, Voting Rights Act 1965.
1. Black migration: Northern and southern cities easier to organise; NAACP (National Association for the Advancement of Colored People) legal challenges; CORE (Congress for Racial Equality) direct action; role of black Christian churches – community relationship; ministers as leaders, e.g. Martin Luther King.
2. Black expectations and education: Soldiers in WWII, fighting for democracy – post-war demand end to discrimination at home; more black education in high schools and

colleges – prepared to act against segregation; other leaders, e.g. Malcolm X; black success in sport and entertainment – baseball, basketball, football, music and films.

3. Cold War: Conflict between democracy and totalitarianism – must end discrimination in US; role of federal government – desegregated the army, enforced laws and decisions of Supreme Court, e.g. Little Rock, Arkansas, James Meredith in University of Mississippi, passed Civil Rights Act and Voting Rights Act; importance of black vote in northern cities.

4. Middle-class whites: Decline of white prejudice – liberal whites in northern cities critical of South; pressure on federal government.

5. Role of mass media: TV, press – publicity for conditions in South – Montgomery Bus Boycott, death of Emmet Till, Selma to Montgomery March, 'Bull' Connor in Birmingham – water hoses on women and children; speeches of Martin Luther King – 'I Have a Dream' speech in Washington.

Conclusion: You could say which factors in your opinion were more important than others and why you think so.

What factors account for the success of black Americans in achieving civil rights in the US?

The answer to this question follows much of the above answer except that you could place more emphasis on **the leadership of Martin Luther King**, e.g. non-violence, speeches, and on campaigns such as the **Montgomery Bus Boycott** and the **Selma to Montgomery March**.

How did Rosa Parks's refusal to give up her bus seat become a victory for Montgomery blacks?

Intro: Jim Crow laws – segregation; buses in Montgomery, Alabama.

1. Rosa Parks: Refused to get up from seat; arrested; fined $10; E.D. Nixon (NAACP) to appeal her case – legal challenge – tactics of NAACP; Nixon not satisfied with character of those arrested before Parks – why Rosa Parks? – personality, member of NAACP, married, working.

2. Use of boycott: Jo Ann Robinson – distribute leaflets – church announcements – one-day boycott – success – continued – further role of churches – meetings, singing, local leadership – Montgomery Improvement Association (MIA) takes over organisation of boycott, led by Martin Luther King.

3. Demands: Jim Crow compromise – black drivers to be employed, drivers courteous, seats filled on a first come, first served basis – refused by bus company – blacks now fight for full integration – organisation of boycott – taxis – lifts – walking – car pool – car insurance.

4. Leadership of Martin Luther King: Role as leader, spokesman, arrested, bombing of home, use of church, became national figure, message of non-violence, peaceful protest, moral and spiritual crusade, favoured full integration, speaker/preacher style.

5. Supreme Court appeal: Long process through lower courts – influence of Chief Justice Earl Warren – decision given in November 1956 – boycott over in December – victory for Montgomery blacks.

Conclusion: You can link the decision of one person (Rosa Parks) to the wider problems of the black community, and how her action led to the mass mobilisation of Montgomery blacks, and reasons for victory.

What was the contribution of the Montgomery Bus Boycott to the civil rights movement?

Intro: Rosa Parks refused to move – arrest – fine – boycott.

1. Leadership of Martin Luther King: Role as leader, spokesman, arrested, bombing of home, use of church, became national figure, message of non-violence, peaceful protest, moral and spiritual crusade, favoured full integration, speaker/preacher style.

2. Direct action, non-violent protest: Boycott in Montgomery, voting registration in Selma; lunch counter protests, freedom riders on interstate buses – force whites to break the law in response.

3. Role of churches: Importance of churches for black community – central focus for blacks who migrated to cities – use of music, prayer; used for meetings – role of black ministers in providing local leadership.

4. Black organisation: NAACP methods – legal challenges – already won in *Brown v. Board of Education, Topeka, Kansas* – later backed students in Little Rock, Arkansas.

5. Role of Supreme Court: Bus company did not give in to demands of bus boycott – decision of Supreme Court resulted in victory – Chief Justice Earl Warren – separate but not equal.

6. Success: Boost to black organisation – gave confidence, pride, further success – Southern Christian Leadership Conference founded by Martin Luther King – umbrella group for later progress.

Conclusion: The federal government had little influence in the Montgomery Bus Boycott, but was very important in other aspects of ending Jim Crow and racial discrimination, e.g. Civil Rights Act, Voting Rights Act, affirmative action.

CASE STUDY: LYNDON JOHNSON AND VIETNAM, 1963–68

How did the US become involved in Vietnam?*

Intro: After WWII – French control of Indochina (Laos, Cambodia, Vietnam) – Truman gave financial help to French against Ho Chi Minh and Vietminh – beginning of US involvement.

1. US view of Vietnam: Cold War in progress – Truman policy of containment (contain communism where it was) – Truman Doctrine – give help to free people fighting spread of communism; growth of McCarthyism – influence on US foreign policy.

2. French out: Dien Bien Phu – Geneva Accords – separate countries – US supported South Vietnam against attacks of Ho Chi Minh – seen as communist, with Soviet and communist Chinese backing; Eisenhower – military advisers to train South Vietnamese army – influenced by domino theory – if South Vietnam fell to communism, others would follow; Kennedy increased advisers to 16,000.

3. Johnson's policies: Influenced by containment, domino theory, relied on Kennedy's advisers, e.g. McNamara – belief in military solution – did not want to be first president to lose a war; decision to withdraw or increase involvement? Tonkin Gulf Incident – Tonkin Resolution – almost unlimited power to wage war; Operation Rolling Thunder against North Vietnam – also more troops – half million by 1968.

Conclusion: Greater involvement in bid to defeat guerrilla warfare; more opposition at home; Tet Offensive – gradual withdrawal – failure of containment.

* See the full essay on 'Why did the US become involved in armed conflict in Vietnam and why did it eventually withdraw from that country?', pp. 173–75.

Why did the US withdraw from Vietnam?*

Intro: Involvement – influenced by policy of containment, domino theory, US credibility – by 1968 heavily involved – but withdrew in 1973. Why?

1. Failure of military solution: US belief in military solution – 'search and destroy' – air bombardments, defoliants, fire-free zones – angered South Vietnamese peasants – failure to win hearts and minds – US failed to see war as nationalist uprising; could not cope with guerrilla warfare; bombing of North Vietnam failed, agricultural economy – corrupt regime in South Vietnam.

2. Anti-war movement: Growth of anti-war movement in US – begun in universities in 1965 – taking resources from Great Society – influence of TV and newspaper reports –

bombing of non-military targets – deaths of Vietnamese civilians; attacks by police on protestors increased anti-war mood.

3. Tet Offensive: Widespread attacks on US and South Vietnamese positions, including US embassy in Saigon – undermined Johnson's claims to be winning the war – growth in anti-war movement – US society polarised – led to Johnson's decision to withdraw from presidential race, begin peace talks in Paris.

4. Nixon's reasons: US economy worsening – wanted to improve relations with communist China – policy of Vietnamisation to shift burden of war – increased anti-war protests because of invasion of Cambodia, e.g. Kent State Massacre.

Conclusion: Peace agreed in Paris – US to withdraw – policy of containment failed – North Vietnam took over South Vietnam in 1975.

* See the full essay on 'Why did the US become involved in armed conflict in Vietnam and why did it eventually withdraw from that country?', pp. 173–75.

To what extent was the Tonkin Gulf Incident a turning point in US policy on Vietnam?

Intro: US involvement – reasons (containment, domino theory, credibility) but gradual involvement – significant involvement by 1968 – was this due to Tonkin Gulf Incident?

1. Gradual involvement: Truman – financial help to French; Eisenhower – money and advisers to South Vietnam; Kennedy – 16,000 advisers and Green Berets – still mainly in South Vietnamese control.

2. Johnson's decision: Withdraw or more involvement? – advisers, e.g. McNamara, belief in military solution – push for greater US involvement; Tonkin Gulf Incident – not serious, some things did not happen – but excuse to increase US involvement – Tonkin Resolution – almost unlimited power to fight war.

3. Increased US involvement: Operation Rolling Thunder – numbers of soldiers, 180,000 by end of 1956, half million by end of 1967 – deaths: less than 2,000 US dead in 1965, more than 14,000 in 1968 – firepower, tonnage of bombs, napalm – big change – US in control of the fighting.

Conclusion: Increased anti-war movement – problems for Great Society – Tet Offensive – another turning point – reversal of previous policy – movement towards peace.

To what extent did the political and military policies of President Johnson lead to greater US involvement in Vietnam?

A similar answer to previous answer **except** change around the paragraphs and add more on the impact of the Tet Offensive.

Intro: Gradual involvement: Truman – financial help to French; Eisenhower – money and advisers to South Vietnam; Kennedy – 16,000 advisers and Green Berets – still mainly in South Vietnamese control.

1. Influences on Johnson: US involvement – reasons – explain containment, domino theory, US credibility – did not want to be first president to lose a war.

2. Johnson's decision: Withdraw or more involvement? – advisers, e.g. McNamara, belief in military solution – push for greater US involvement; Tonkin Gulf Incident – not serious, some things did not happen – but excuse to increase US involvement – Tonkin Resolution – almost unlimited power to fight war.

3. Increased US involvement: Operation Rolling Thunder – numbers of soldiers, 180,000 by end of 1956, half million by end 1967 – deaths: less than 2,000 US dead in 1965, more than 14,000 in 1968 – firepower, tonnage of bombs, napalm – big change – US in control of the fighting.

4. Tet Offensive 1968: Reversal of previous Johnson policy – reduction in US involvement – will not contest presidential election – began process which led to peace – Paris Peace talks.

Conclusion: Make a judgment on the extent to which you think Johnson's policies led to greater US involvement.

What was the impact of the Vietnam War on the Johnson presidency?

Intro: Gradual involvement from Truman to Kennedy – Johnson's policies escalate US involvement in Vietnam – most intense period from 1966 to 1968.

1. Greater involvement in war: Said little about the war in first year so as not to endanger chances of election – campaigned as candidate of peace against Barry Goldwater; Johnson involved in war day and night – distracted from other foreign policy issues and domestic policy issues.

2. Anti-war movement: Growth of anti-war movement in US – begun in universities in 1965 – influence of TV and newspaper reports – bombing of non-military targets – deaths of Vietnamese civilians; attacks by police on protestors increased anti-war mood – Tet Offensive – widespread attacks on US and South Vietnamese positions – undermined

Johnson's claims to be winning the war – growth in anti-war movement – US society polarised – 'credibility gap' – led to Johnson's decision to withdraw from presidential race, begin peace talks in Paris.

3. Great Society: Vietnam distracted from Great Society – had regrets about involvement – that 'bitch of a war' because it took him away from 'the woman he really loved' (the Great Society) – most Great Society proposals passed before serious involvement in Vietnam – little later in presidency – Vietnam used resources that could have been used in Great Society – Vietnam War in total cost twenty times more than all programmes on Great Society – Martin Luther King – 'promises of Great Society shot dead in the battlefields of Vietnam'.

4. Increased power for president: Tonkin Gulf Resolution – enlarged powers of presidency – growth towards imperial presidency – mistrust after Tet Offensive – later Pentagon papers show government lying and abuse of power over Vietnam – Congress wanted to rein in presidential powers – did so during Nixon presidency.

Conclusion: Economy got boost during Johnson presidency because of spending on war (and tax cuts) – unemployment fell – but problems later – growth in budget deficit; inflation begun but more serious later.

CASE STUDY: THE MOON LANDING, 1969

Why did the US plan a moon landing during the 1960s?

Intro: In 1969, *Apollo 11* landed on the moon – end of programme which included Mercury, Gemini and Apollo projects – organised by NASA – why?

1. Cold War competition: Cold War – competition between capitalism and communism; Soviet success – first rocket, first man in space – US disappointment; Kennedy – man on the moon by end of decade; development of rocketry needed for nuclear attack; danger of attack from space – US won the race to the moon – national pride – most powerful country.

2. NASA propaganda: Use of press, radio and television – message of excitement of space exploration, value to economy, Cold War competition, superiority of US technology; example – documentaries, *The John Glenn Story* (1963), produced by NASA, also documentary on use of computers in space exploration; to ensure public support and congressional funding for space programme – CIA intelligence on Soviet space shots used by NASA to persuade Congress – NASA had to counter bad publicity of fire in *Apollo 7* and deaths of three astronauts.

3. Role of media: Get message across – convince taxpayers of validity of paying for moon landing; link to Cold War; NASA controlled information to newspapers, TV spectaculars of launches and of shots on moon and moon landing, photographs, press releases – media willing to co-operate because of patriotism – but some critics, especially after *Apollo 7*.

4. Boost for economy: $25 billion – 400,000 jobs – prosperity for Sun Belt states, especially Florida (Cape Kennedy), Texas (Houston) and California; improved technology; military–industrial complex.

Conclusion: You can make a judgment on which causes you think were the most important, and why.

How did advances in technology contribute to the moon landing in 1969?

Intro: Space exploration – 1950s NASA set up – Cold War competition; President Kennedy's speech – man on moon by end of the decade – motivation; technology the means to get to moon.

1. Advances in rockets/missiles: Nuclear war, ICBM – Atlas, Titan rockets, Cold War rivalry, role of military–industrial complex.

2. Space technology: Challenge to US technology, projects to overcome obstacles to moon landing, Mercury Project – Shepard, Glenn – three orbits.

3. Gemini projects: Two-man space flights, rendezvous and docking, space walks, *Surveyor* space flights – testing and photographing surface of moon, *Lunar Orbiter* – photo sites.

4. Apollo mission: Testing Saturn rocket, three-man spacecraft, setback with *Apollo 7* – three die, *Apollo 8* – orbit of moon and return, TV, *Apollo 9* – docking, *10* – lunar module tested.

5. Moon landing: *Apollo 11*, three stages, most powerful rocket, three astronauts, simulators, weightlessness, spacesuits, freeze-dried food, use of lunar module, scientific experiments, heat shield, computers.

Conclusion: Huge project – 400,000 employees, $25 billion, US ahead of Soviet technology, later landings, space stations and shuttle, later Star Wars.

To what extent do you agree with the view that the success of the moon landing in 1969 was due as much to human skill as to technological development?

Introduction: Mention the moon landing and the background to it. The main answer to this question would show the role of both technological development and human skill in the success of the moon landing. But because the question says 'to what extent…', you can argue that it was mainly technology **or** mainly human skill **or** an equal combination of both.

1. Role of technological development: Advances in rockets/missiles – nuclear war, ICBM – Atlas, Titan rockets, role of military–industrial complex – space technology: challenge to US technology, projects to overcome obstacles to moon landing, Mercury Project – Shepard, Glenn – three orbits, some failures of technology – *Apollo 7* – three die; success of *Apollo 11*.

2. Human skill – role of astronauts: Three astronauts – skilled pilots – Armstrong, Korean War pilot, a test pilot X-15 rocket plane – Aldrin, Korean War pilot – Collins pilot – rendezvous and docking techniques.

3. Landing: Problems – computer overload – manual guidance of lunar module by Armstrong to select a good site; decisions at control centre – to abort or not – judgment to continue; take-off – problems with broken switch – solved by Aldrin with pen.

Conclusion: Make your final assessment as to the balance between technology and human skill in achieving success on the moon landing.

What was the impact of space exploration on the US?

Introduction: Give a brief summary of space exploration from the 1950s to the 1980s. Then the main part of the answer must assess what impacts/effects space exploration had on the US.

1. Fight the Cold War: Main concerns – Vietnam War, the economy, counterculture, divisions – space exploration mostly successful, boost to US pride, morale, more advanced than the Soviet Union.

2. Boost to economy: $25 billion – 400,000 jobs – prosperity for Sun Belt states, especially Florida (Cape Kennedy), Texas (Houston) and California; improved technology – weather and communications (TV, phone lines) satellites – tiny instruments, e.g. cameras for operating – silicon chip for computers, etc.; military–industrial complex.

3. Great Society: Cost of space exploration – not as serious as Vietnam War – slow down Great Society – contribute to federal deficits.

4. Role of media: Get message across – convince taxpayers of validity of paying for moon landing; link to Cold War; NASA controlled information to newspapers, TV spectaculars of shots on moon and moon landing – movies, such as *2001: Space Odyssey*.

Conclusion: You can decide whether space exploration was worth the cost, or did the positive effects outweigh the negative effects?

POLITICS AND SOCIETY IN NORTHERN IRELAND, 1949–93

A Framework for the Case Studies

Each of the Case Studies has links to Elements in the Topics. It is important to study both the relevant Elements as well as the Case Study.

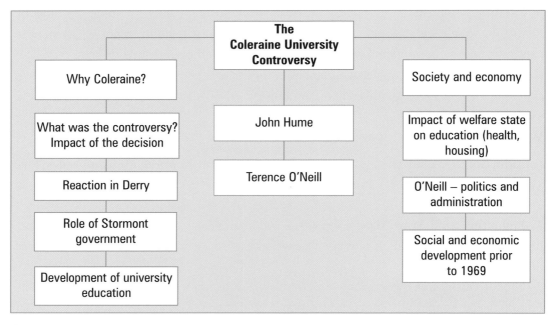

The
Coleraine University Controversy

Why Coleraine?

What was the controversy?
Impact of the decision

Reaction in Derry

Role of Stormont
government

Development of university
education

John Hume

Terence O'Neill

Society and economy

Impact of welfare state
on education (health,
housing)

O'Neill – politics and
administration

Social and economic
development prior
to 1969

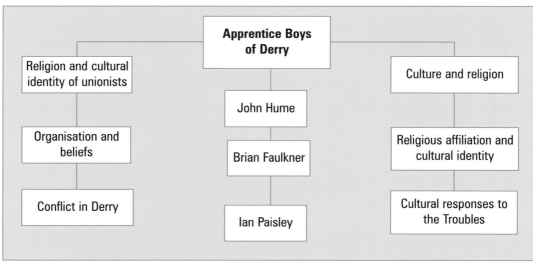

**Apprentice Boys
of Derry**

Religion and cultural
identity of unionists

Organisation and
beliefs

Conflict in Derry

John Hume

Brian Faulkner

Ian Paisley

Culture and religion

Religious affiliation and
cultural identity

Cultural responses to
the Troubles

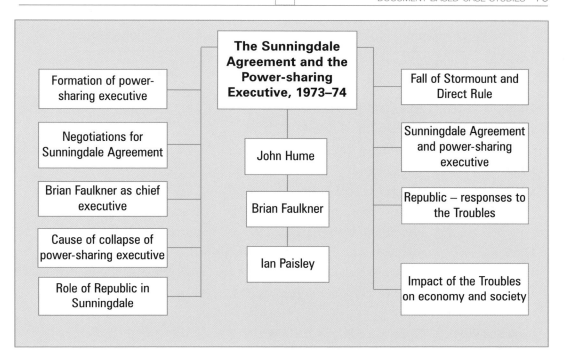

The Sunningdale Agreement and the Power-sharing Executive, 1973–74

Formation of power-sharing executive

Negotiations for Sunningdale Agreement

Brian Faulkner as chief executive

Cause of collapse of power-sharing executive

Role of Republic in Sunningdale

John Hume

Brian Faulkner

Ian Paisley

Fall of Stormount and Direct Rule

Sunningdale Agreement and power-sharing executive

Republic – responses to the Troubles

Impact of the Troubles on economy and society

NORTHERN IRELAND CASE STUDIES – TIMELINE

1689	Siege and Relief of Derry.
1690	Battle of the Boyne.
1714	Apprentice Boys of Derry founded.
1947	Education Act.
1963	Terence O'Neill Prime Minister.
1964	Lockwood Committee on Higher Education in Northern Ireland appointed. University for Derry Committee founded.
1965	Lockwood Committee report published.
1967	Northern Ireland Civil Rights Association (NICRA) founded.
1969	Terence O'Neill resigned as PM, succeeded by James Chichester-Clark.
August 1969	Apprentice Boys parade in Derry.
August 1969	Battle of the Bogside.
March 1972	Direct Rule from Westminster imposed on Northern Ireland.
December 1973	Sunningdale Conference and Agreement.
January 1974	Power-sharing executive in operation. Faulkner resigned as leader of Ulster Unionist Party.
February 1974	British general election.
May 1974	Ulster Workers Council strike. Collapse of power-sharing executive.
1984	Amalgamation of Ulster Polytechnic and New University of Ulster to form University of Ulster.
1986	Apprentice Boys march in Garvaghy Road, Portadown, riots.

Case Study: The Coleraine University Controversy

SAMPLE QUESTION 1

Document A

The Lockwood Committee report on the qualities of the site needed for the second university.

> It is of prime importance that the second university should have a site of adequate magnitude [size] to accommodate its proposed activities and to allow for future growth. ... In view of the importance of residential accommodation to university life, ample provision of space for halls of residence, college houses and student flats should be made in planning. ... A site of about 300 acres might be thought sufficient for a new university which is planned to grow to some 6,000 students, but if the new university is to develop fully the activities which we propose, particularly in agriculture, very much more space than this will be required. ... It is of paramount importance in our view that, as the university develops, it should be able to do so within the boundaries of a single site.

Source: *Lockwood Committee Report on Higher Education in Northern Ireland*, Her Majesty's Stationery Office, Belfast, 1965.

Document B

The Lockwood Committee report on existing facilities at Magee College.

> Magee College occupies a pleasant situation on a site of about 20 acres... The main building contains lecture rooms, the library and the common room. The refectory, departmental and administrative premises, some student hostels and staff houses are also within the College precinct. Other students' hostels are within a few minutes' walk of the main College building. Teaching accommodation is being strained by the increasing numbers of full-time students. Science courses have been introduced only recently and very limited science facilities are supplemented by sharing some laboratories in the Londonderry Municipal Technical College and Londonderry High School...in the library there are reading places for only about 70 students and 12 staff...in 1963/64 there were 245 undergraduates (153 men and 92 women) enrolled.

Source: *Lockwood Committee Report on Higher Education in Northern Ireland*, Her Majesty's Stationery Office, Belfast, 1965.

1. (a) Why is a site of adequate size needed, according to Document A?

   (b) How large a site does the report suggest?

   (c) How large is the site at Magee College, according to Document B?

   (d) Where does Magee College supplement its science facilities?

   (e) How many students did Magee College have in 1963–64?

2. (a) What criteria for an adequate site outlined in Document A are not fulfilled in Document B?

   (b) How much smaller was Magee College (Document B) compared to the proposed second university (Document A)?

3. (a) What are the limitations of these sources for analysing the reasons why the Lockwood Committee decided against Magee College as the site of the second university?

   (b) Is there evidence of bias in the writing of these sources? Explain your answer.

4. What were the conclusions of the Lockwood Committee in relation to a second university for Northern Ireland?

SAMPLE QUESTION 2

Document A

Derry prepares for 'Siege of Stormont'
Orange and Green united in protest

By Andrew Hamilton

Derry's people – Catholic and Protestant – will unite in protest against the decision which rejected its claim to the proposed new university. On Thursday morning, a motorcade, which it is confidently expected will include three or four thousand cars, will drive 90 miles to Stormont... Unionist and Nationalist citizens of Derry's 60,000 population are supporting the city's case for the new university. The shops will close on Thursday to release employees for the protest. ... Derry people yesterday expressed the feeling that they, and the north-west area of Tyrone and Fermanagh, were not being treated fairly... Derry's claim for the university was submitted for the Lockwood Committee by a corporation sub-committee. But even more significant was the formation a few weeks ago of the University for Derry Committee... [Mr Patrick Gormley, Nationalist MP for Mid-Ulster said], 'Derry suffered with partition for it was shorn of its natural hinterland – Donegal. ... We are creating a brain drain from the city if the university does not come here. People are looking to the future and naturally they will be attracted to a university town.'

Source: *The Irish Times*, 16 February 1965.

Document B

The Lockwood Committee report on the reasons why the Coleraine area satisfied its criteria.

In our concerted view the Coleraine area satisfies our criteria better than any of the other areas we have considered. ... This area alone can provide the residential facilities which must be available in the critical years immediately ahead. ... It has a background distinctively different from the background against which Queen's University is set, and for that reason is eminently suitable for the establishment of the different kind of university which we recommend, and for the new developments in the education of teachers such as will characterise the Education Centre. ... It is also an area which would attract first-rate staff, and can offer housing accommodation to rent on a short-term basis and good sites on which to bailiff. It is, nevertheless, convenient to Belfast, and to Northern Ireland's civil airport at Aldergrove...conferences and seminars should flourish there as ample accommodation will be available for academic visitors. We are satisfied that the sponsoring local authorities are able and willing to support the establishment of a university...

Source: *Lockwood Committee Report on Higher Education in Northern Ireland*, Her Majesty's Stationery Office, Belfast, 1965.

1. (a) According to Document A, why were Catholics and Protestants in Derry united?
   (b) How many cars are expected to drive to Stormont?
   (c) Who submitted Derry's claim for a university to the Lockwood Committee?
   (d) What attractions does the Coleraine area offer in relation to housing accommodation, according to Document B?
   (e) Where is the Coleraine area convenient to?
2. (a) What arguments are put forward in Document A which are not considered in Document B?
   (b) What criteria are used in Document B which are not mentioned in Document A?
3. (a) What are the differences in the style of the two sources, A and B? Explain your answer.
   (b) Do both sources, A and B, show evidence of bias and propaganda?
4. What were the arguments for and against siting the new university at Coleraine?

SAMPLE QUESTION 3

Document A

> ### Derry's protest trek to Stormont
>
> A protest procession of 2,000 cars arrived in Belfast yesterday carrying public representatives of every section of opinion in Derry. They were objecting to the Northern Ireland Government's decision to establish the second university of the area in Coleraine instead of Derry. ... Before leaving Derry, The Mayor, Councillor Anderson (Unionist) said, 'We are demonstrating the unanimous feeling in this city and in Co. Tyrone, and I believe, in Co. Fermanagh, behind our claim.' He added: 'Derry has a flourishing university college. It should be developed immediately. We have nothing against Coleraine but we believe the Government's decision is not the correct one in recommending Coleraine in preference to Derry as the site.' Mr John Hume, chairman of the University for Derry Action Committee, said, 'The Lockwood Committee's terms of reference did not include the question of a site and this question was explicitly placed outside the terms of reference...Derry is the second city in Northern Ireland, and the only centre of population, outside Belfast, large enough to absorb the student life of a modern university.'

Source: *The Irish Times*, 19 February 1965.

Document B

An historian's account of the meeting between the Lockwood Committee and the delegation from Derry presenting its case for a new university.

> Lockwood and his colleagues initially handled the Londonderry councillors with far greater care. The Committee seemed interested primarily in getting the councillors' views on Magee's possible relationship with the new university should it be sited in Derry. The councillors were well aware of the various oddities of Magee's administrative structure; in one degree or other all of them felt that the College could serve only as a base or launching-pad from which the new institution could develop. Thereafter '...it might be turned into a teacher-training college or anything at all. It doesn't matter. You are taking from it the best use you possibly can.' (Councillor Austin) As Venables [Lockwood Committee member] tried to persuade the councillors to consider scenarios [situations] for the new university that did not involve Magee the discussion became heated. Despite the apparent indifference of

the councillors to the long-term fate of the College they seemed to regard it as the embodiment of Derry's historical claim to be 'The Site'...

Source: Gerard O'Brien, 'Our Magee Problem: Stormont and the Second University', in *Derry and Londonderry, History and Society*, Gerard O'Brien (ed.), Geography Publications, Dublin.

1. (a) How many cars went on the protest procession to Belfast, according to Document A?
   (b) Who was mayor of Derry?
   (c) What was the second city in Northern Ireland?
   (d) What could happen to Magee College, according to Councillor Austin. in Document B?
   (e) What was Venables trying to persuade the councillors to consider?
2. (a) What evidence is there in Document A which would support the view of Document B that the councillors regarded Magee College as 'the embodiment of Derry's claim to the be "The Site"'?
   (b) What views expressed in Document B would undermine John Hume's view in Document A that the 'Lockwood Committee's terms of reference did not include the question of a site'?
3. (a) What advantage(s) has an historian (such as in Document B) over a journalist (such as in Document A) in analysing the events surrounding the Coleraine University controversy?
   (b) How do the aims of the speakers in Document A differ from the author of Document B?
4. Why was there controversy because of the choice of Coleraine as the site of a new university?

SAMPLE QUESTION 4

Document A

John Hume speaking at a meeting in London organised by the Campaign for Democracy in Ulster (CDU), an all-party coalition of MPs dominated by Labour MPs of the centre-left of the party.

Hume outlined the economic and political background of the Lockwood scandal pointing out that none of the members of the inquiry committee was a Catholic. He asserted: 'Not a single academic criterion is to be found in the report for the choice of Coleraine.' ... 'The minority in Northern Ireland resides mainly in the western counties of Derry, Tyrone and Fermanagh. To develop these areas is to develop areas opposed to the government and to lose the few Unionist seats held there. The plan is therefore to develop the strongly Unionist Belfast–Coleraine–Portadown triangle and to cause a migration from West to East "Ulster", redistributing and scattering the minority so that the Unionist Party will not only maintain but strengthen its position. The British taxpayer is paying for these schemes... Yet it would appear that the British Treasury doles out this [money] without attempting to scrutinise in any detail the uses to which it is put.'

Source: Paul Routledge, *John Hume, A Biography*, HarperCollins Publishers, London, 1997.

Document B

An historian's account of the factors which influenced the Lockwood Committee in making its decision on siting the new university.

The facts indicate that the Lockwood Committee made its decision on the location of the university on the basis of practices long accepted as sound with regard to the establishment of new British universities. This – all unknown to the English members Lockwood, Jackson and Venables who largely 'led' the rest of the Committee – was where the logic of the decision failed. Economic, social and cultural conditions in Ulster were not those which obtained elsewhere in Britain. Tensions underlay the competition for the university between Derry and Coleraine which were far removed from the sort of rivalry with which Lockwood was more familiar...and almost certainly had no proper appreciation... The unpalatable [disagreeable] notion that the Coleraine promoters had done their research more thoroughly deserves recognition. Likewise the 'faceless men', now a euphemism for all supposed Unionist double-dealing and bigotry, turned out to have been rather less malignant [nasty] than the legend would have us believe.

Source: Gerard O'Brien, 'Our Magee Problem: Stormont and the Second University', in *Derry and Londonderry, History and Society*, Gerard O'Brien (ed.), Geography Publications, Dublin.

1. (a) How many members of the Lockwood Committee were Catholics, according to Document A?

   (b) Where does the minority in Northern Ireland mainly reside, according to John Hume?

   (c) What is 'the plan', according to John Hume in Document A?

   (d) Who were the English members of the Lockwood Committee, according to Document B?

   (e) What is the term 'faceless men' used for, according to Document B?

2. (a) Is there any information provided in Document B which could be used to support the case made in Document A?

   (b) What information in Document A shows what 'tensions underlay the competition for the university between Derry and Coleraine' (Document B)?

3. (a) What advantage does the historian in Document B have over John Hume in Document A in assessing the factors which led to the Lockwood Committee's decisions?

   (b) Do you think the historian in Document B agrees with the views of John Hume in Document A in relation to the reasons for siting the university in Coleraine?

4. What part did Terence O'Neill and/or John Hume play in the Coleraine University controversy?

OTHER CONTEXTUAL QUESTIONS ON THE COLERAINE UNIVERSITY CONTROVERSY

1. What did the Coleraine University controversy contribute to the beginning of the civil rights campaign in Northern Ireland?

2. To what extent were the accusations of bias and discrimination against the Lockwood Committee unfounded?

3. Was the Lockwood Committee another example of discrimination by the Unionist government of the area west of the Bann?

Case Study: The Apprentice Boys of Derry

SAMPLE QUESTION 1

Document A

Who Are the Apprentice Boys of Derry?

The Apprentice Boys of Derry are an historical association whose members are committed to maintaining the spirit of liberty displayed by the Apprentice Boys in 1688 against oppression. The Apprentice Boys perpetuate that spirit of liberty, inherent to the Reformed Protestant faith, by faithfully commemorating the 'Derry Celebrations' within the Maiden City and in other localities, keeping alive the memory of the Brave 13 and the heroic sacrifices of the besieged within the Walls… Each year the Apprentice Boys of Derry celebrate two dates in the city of Londonderry. First, the closing of the City gates by thirteen young Apprentices against the enemy forces on 18th December. And second, when the City was relieved after the Siege, having held out and not surrendered despite about 10,000 of the defenders dying in Her defence, on 12th August.

These celebrations take the form of a parade by the organisation to and from a Church Service held in the historic Saint Columb's, Church of Ireland (Anglican) Cathedral. The organisation has some 10,000 members, who converge on Londonderry to take part in the commemorative parade through the City.

Source: ABODonline, About Us, www.apprenticeboys.co.uk.

Document B

Who Are the Apprentice Boys?

At the start of the siege of Londonderry in 1689, 13 apprentice boys slammed the city gates against the army of the Catholic King James II.

The Apprentice Boys of Derry, one of the Protestant Loyal Orders, is based upon this defiant action of 'no surrender'.

New Apprentice Boys can only be initiated inside the city, in ceremonies in August and December each year.

The order holds its main parade in Derry on 12 August to celebrate the relief of the city and the end of the siege.

Usually some 10,000–12,000 members take part.

There is a lesser demonstration on 18 December, to mark the shutting of the gates, when an effigy is burned of Colonel Lundy, an officer who tried to negotiate the surrender of the city in 1689. Even today those regarded as traitors to the unionist cause can be referred to as 'Lundies'.

Source: BBC News, Saturday, 14 August 1999, www.bbc.co.uk.

1. (a) According to Document A, what are the Apprentice Boys committed to maintaining?
   (b) Who are the Brave 13 mentioned in Document A?
   (c) Where do the Apprentice Boys hold church services on the days they parade?
   (d) According to Document B, where are new Apprentice Boys initiated?
   (e) Who are 'Lundies'?
2. (a) Select three pieces of information on which Document A and Document B agree.
   (b) What information is given in Document B which is not given in Document A?
3. (a) Is there evidence of bias in Document A? Explain your answer.
   (b) Which document, A or B, would you regard as more reliable? Explain your answer.
4. What was the contribution of the Apprentice Boys of Derry to the celebration of religious and cultural identity among the city's unionist minority?

SAMPLE QUESTION 2

Document A

An account of the Apprentice Boys of Derry organisation.

The Apprentice Boys of Derry was founded in its present form in 1814. If the Orange Institution has the Battle of the Boyne as its main commemorative event, the Apprentice Boys have the Siege of Derry from 1688 to 1689. Whilst the Apprentice Boys share the Protestant religious ethos of the Orange Order, the central purpose of the organisation is to commemorate the Siege. Apprentice Boys wear a distinctive crimson collarette and usually carry bannerettes rather than large banners. The City of Londonderry is seen as so important that anyone wishing to become an Apprentice Boy must be initiated within the city walls. The organisation is divided into eight 'parent clubs': Baker, Browning, Campsie, Mitchelbourne, Murray, Walker, the Apprentice Boys of Derry Club and the No Surrender Club. Affiliated to one of these clubs are a series of branch clubs organised through Ireland, Scotland, England and beyond.

Source: Dominic Bryan, *Orange Parades: The Politics of Ritual, Tradition and Control*, Pluto Press, London, 2000.

Document B

An analysis of what the Apprentice Boys parades represent.

Londonderry has long been the most potent [powerful] symbolic place in Ulster for unionists, and the story of the siege remains the most powerful metaphor [symbol, image] of Protestant sensibilities in Ireland. The narrative [story] is used to illustrate the need for decisive action, for unity in adversity [difficult times]; and it can be used as a justification for resistance to the law. It is used also as a warning of the danger of compromise and to justify the fear of the traitor within. Parading the walls of Derry is not just about maintaining tradition and celebrating loyalist culture, it is also about reaffirming the principles on which Protestant power was structured in Ulster: never trust the enemy within, exclude them from power and authority.

But Derry is also a city in which Catholics have long been the majority of the population. Under Stormont, gerrymandering of the local government wards ensured that Unionists retained control of the city council. The city therefore had a special significance for the nationalists too: it was a symbol of their second-class status in Northern Ireland.

Source: Neil Jarman, *Material Conflicts, Parades and Visual Displays in Northern Ireland*, Berg, Oxford, 1997.

1. (a) According to Document A, when was the Apprentice Boys of Derry founded?
    (b) What regalia do the Apprentice Boys wear or carry on parades?
    (c) How many 'parent clubs' form the Apprentice Boys?
    (d) From Document B, give one example of what the story of the Siege of Derry is used by the Apprentice Boys to illustrate.
    (e) How did unionists retain control of the city council of Derry, according to Document B?

2. (a) Do you think the information in Document A supports the view in Document B that 'Londonderry has long been the most potent symbolic place in Ulster for unionists'?
    (b) Which aspect of Document B is not referred to in Document A?

3. (a) Which document, A or B, is more factual? Explain your answer.
    (b) What would you need to know about the provenance (origins) of both of these sources to assess them for usefulness and reliability?

4. What contribution did the Apprentice Boys of Derry make to the development of a cultural identity for unionists in Northern Ireland?

SAMPLE QUESTION 3

Document A

A biographer's view of John Hume's role before the Apprentice Boys parade in Derry, August 1969.

Hume knew the lid could blow off in Derry if the annual march of the Apprentice Boys were to go ahead, so he made direct approaches to both the Dublin and British Governments to head off the catastrophe. The Taoiseach, Jack Lynch, listened politely to this articulate MP, who was becoming a familiar face on Irish television, but since there was already a Northern 'expert', Agriculture Minister Neil Blaney, from just across the border in Donegal, Hume's views were not given full weight. In London, Hume was unable to see James Callaghan [Home Secretary], and was fobbed off with a ten-minute meeting with Lord Stonham, his deputy at the Home Office, which extended into a 3 hour lunch... He succeeded in impressing Stonham with his fears about the march, and these were reported up the line to Prime Minister Harold Wilson. But again Hume's opinions were regarded as alarmist, and London was persuaded not to intervene, after meeting strenuous opposition from Belfast.

Source: Barry White, *John Hume*, Blackstaff Press, Belfast, 1985.

Document B

An historian's view of the background to the Apprentice Boys parade in Derry, August 1969.

There was mounting anxiety in official circles about the imminent Apprentice Boys parade in Derry. Robert Porter, the home affairs minister [in Stormont], was reluctant to impose a ban, and when Hume travelled to London to express his fears to the Home Office, he was considered unduly alarmist. Since most of its demands had been met, The Derry Citizens' Action Committee was in abeyance but it was supplanted by the more militant Derry Citizens Defence Association which, though it promised it would do nothing to provoke trouble, was led by Sean Keenan, widely understood to be a former IRA activist. With memories of the police invasion after Burntollet still fresh in their minds, the people of the Bogside prepared for a siege and, as arsenals of petrol bombs were prepared, the main roads into the district were barricaded with scaffolding, paving stones, planks and furniture.

Source: Jonathan Bardon, *A History of Ulster*, Blackstaff Press, Belfast, 2001.

1. (a) In Document A, whom does Hume approach to 'head off the catastrophe'?

    (b) Why was John Hume becoming familiar?

    (c) Who did Hume meet in London?

    (d) According to Document B, how were Hume's opinions viewed in London?

    (e) What preparations did the people of the Bogside make for a siege?

2. (a) Do Documents A and B agree on the role of John Hume?

    (b) What information does Document B give which supports the views that 'the lid could blow off in Derry' (Document A)?

3. (a) Is the author of the biography in Document A favourable to Hume? Explain your answer.

    (b) Does the author of Document B suggest that the 'trouble' was planned?

4. What aspects of the Apprentice Boys tradition were causes of conflict with Catholics and nationalists in Derry?

SAMPLE QUESTION 4

Document A

Prayers for Peace in Derry Churches

Catholics issue warning

Prayers were offered in all Derry churches yesterday for peace tomorrow when members of the Apprentice Boys' Order and their supporters from every part of the North will be celebrating the raising of the Siege of 1689.

   The Apprentice Boys' Order was founded in memory of the 13 youths who locked the gates of the old walled city against Catholic James II. The relief came when a man-o'-war with supplies broke a boom across the Foyle when the siege was in its 105th day.

   A quiet, brooding calm enveloped the city yesterday. ... In one street the quiet was broken by the hammering of workmen putting up a net-wire shuttering on a shop window. The shop is along the three-mile processional route over which about 5,000 Apprentice Boys will be marching accompanied by about 100 bands.

   In the afternoon more than 1,000 people gathered in Celtic GAA Park to listen to appeals for peace but also a warning that the Catholics of the Bogside would defend themselves if attacked... The attendance included a large proportion of teenagers.

Source: *The Irish Times*, 11 August 1969.

Document B

Violence erupts again in Derry

Hopes for sectarian peace perished in Derry yesterday as street violence flared in the wake of the traditional Apprentice Boys march through the centre of the city.

It began with an act of stone-throwing by Catholic youths as the Protestant parade passed the Guildhall place. The stones came thicker despite efforts by civil rights stewards and political leaders, including Mr John Hume, MP, Mr Eddie McAteer, and Mr Eamon McCann. Quickly it spread into a bitter running battle between RUC riot squads and groups of men and youths from the Bogside.

Men, women and policemen were struck down under the continuous hail of bricks and stones. Petrol-bombs rained from side-streets as the police advanced. Buildings were set ablaze.

Late into last night the fighting continued. The RUC behind a wall of shields and gas-masks advanced and fired tear-gas bombs into the rioters.

Source: *The Irish Times*, 13 August 1969.

1. (a) Why were prayers offered in all Derry churches, according to Document A?
    (b) What happened to break the quiet in one street in Derry?
    (c) What was the message of the speakers in Celtic GAA Park?
    (d) What began the street violence, according to Document B?
    (e) Who tried to stop the street violence?
2. (a) Is the warning of Document A 'that the Catholics of the Bogside would defend themselves if attacked' supported by the events described in Document B?
    (b) Did the shopkeeper who put up the net-wire shuttering (Document A) make the right decision?
3. (a) Using evidence from Documents A and/or B, how do the documents illustrate the strengths and weaknesses of newspaper reports as sources for historians?
    (b) Is there any evidence from the documents to show that the newspaper reports are trying to be balanced and fair-minded?
4. Why were the activities of the Apprentice Boys a source of tension in Derry City?

OTHER CONTEXTUAL QUESTIONS ON THE APPRENTICE BOYS OF DERRY

1. 'Divided societies are sometimes culturally productive.' How true is this statement of Northern Ireland from 1949 to 1993?
2. What part did the Apprentice Boys of Derry play in the affairs of Northern Ireland?
3. How did the Apprentice Boys of Derry reflect religious affiliation and cultural identity in Northern Ireland between 1949 and 1993?

Case Study: The Sunningdale Agreement and the Power-sharing Executive

SAMPLE QUESTION 1

Document A

White Paper Heralds New Deal for North

Minority to share power in 80-seat Assembly; election by P.R.

But Westminster to retain control of Law and Justice

From James Downey, Our London Editor

The British Government's White Paper, 'Northern Ireland Constitutional Proposals', published yesterday, proposes the setting up of an 80-seat Assembly, which will be elected by Proportional Representation, and whose executive power will be shared by the Catholic minority.

Summary of Proposals

*   The present status of Northern Ireland as part of the United Kingdom will continue to be guaranteed so long as the majority of its inhabitants so desire.
*   Responsibility for the security forces for the administration of justice and for special powers will remain with Westminster.
*   A new Northern Ireland Assembly, elected by Proportional Representation, will develop its own rules... Discussions will be held...to arrive at an acceptable basis for the formation of an Executive.
*   There will be a Charter of Human Rights, with stringent legislative safeguards.
*   The British Government is prepared to facilitate the setting up of a Council of Ireland, which may be inter-parliamentary as well as inter-Governmental. It proposes to call a conference representative of Westminster, Dublin and the new Assembly to discuss the question.

Source: *The Irish Times*, 21 March 1973.

Document B

> **Unionists seek talks in London**
>
> **Many loyalists displeased at proposals**
>
> The Unionist Party is to seek urgent negotiations with the British Government in a bid to change what it describes as 'unacceptable' proposals contained in the White Paper... The party leader, Mr Brian Faulkner, is expected to meet some of his Westminster Unionist colleagues to finalise a united-front approach to the British Government... Mr Craig [leader of the Vanguard Party] said that the White Paper was 'the worst of all worlds as far as we are concerned. It neither gives us strong parliamentary government in terms of Northern Ireland, nor does it give us effective integration with the United Kingdom.' As there has been no return to a meaningful Stormont, he would make government in Northern Ireland unworkable.

Source: *The Irish Times*, 21 March 1973.

1. (a) How many seats were in the proposed Assembly, according to Document A?
   (b) What was the title of the British government's White Paper?
   (c) What type of council is the British government prepared to facilitate?
   (d) What did the Unionist Party think of the proposals in the British government's White Paper, according to Document B?
   (e) Who was the leader of the Vanguard Party?
2. (a) What aspects of the British government's White Paper as reported in Document A would Mr Craig regard as not giving 'us strong parliamentary government in terms of Northern Ireland'?
   (b) In what way are the proposals of Document A the opposite to 'effective integration' (Document B)?
3. (a) Using evidence from Documents A and/or B, what are the advantages or strengths of newspapers as sources for historians?
   (b) Do the headings and subheadings of the stories accurately reflect the contents of the stories? Explain your answer.
4. What factors contributed to the formation of a power-sharing executive in Northern Ireland, 1973–74?

SAMPLE QUESTION 2

Document A

Maurice Hayes, civil servant, was educated at Queen's University Belfast before becoming town clerk of Downpatrick and eventually Ombudsman for Northern Ireland. He acted as adviser to and author of a number of commissions and reports.

Sunningdale was an uneasy starting point for the Executive. In one sense it identified the opposition: everybody who was not here. This included the rump of non-Faulkner Unionists, Vanguard, Paisley, and the IRA. All of them had a vested interest in bringing it down... Another difficulty about Sunningdale was that while the Irish and British delegations formed coherent and separate entities...the parties of the Executive went separately. There was no single Executive view... In particular, while the SDLP more or less secured the support of the Irish Government, Faulkner did not have the backing of the British when he most needed it. Faulkner himself was a naturally optimistic man, confident of his ability to make a deal, and also sure of his ability to sell it afterwards. There is now plenty of evidence that he was pushed further than he should have been, and beyond his power to deliver. It is also clear that on crucial issues, instead of backing Faulkner, Heath joined the others in putting pressure on him.

Source: Maurice Hayes, *Minority Verdict, Experiences of a Catholic Public Servant*, Blackstaff Press, Belfast, 1995.

Document B

Faulkner Defeat
Unionists reject Sunningdale agreement by 80-vote margin
New Party may emerge from Split
By Conor O'Clery and Walter Ellis

More than 800 constituency and Orange delegates to the Ulster Unionist Council yesterday rejected by 80 votes the Sunningdale agreement on a Council of Ireland after five hours of bitter debate behind the closed doors of the Ulster Hall in Belfast. The vote is a personal defeat for the party leader, Mr Brian Faulkner. He said last night, however, that his policies would remain unchanged and he would continue to lead the Unionist Party and the new Northern Ireland Executive. Both his supporters and opponents in the party concede that his unexpectedly heavy defeat has made the formation of a new Unionist Party under Mr Faulkner now almost inevitable. Unpledged Unionists were jubilant as they filed out of the Ulster Hall... Mr John Taylor, Assembly member for Fermanagh–South Tyrone, who moved the motion 'that this Ulster Unionist Council rejects the proposed all-Ireland Council settlement', said that a meeting of the party's Standing Committee must now be called to decide the leadership of the party.

Source: *The Irish Times*, 5 January 1974.

1. (a) According to Document A, what groups had a vested interest in bringing down Sunningdale?
   (b) To whom did the Irish government give their support?
   (c) What was Heath's attitude to Faulkner?
   (d) What was the voting margin against the Sunningdale Agreement in the Ulster Unionist Council, according to Document B?
   (e) What is likely to happen because of the split in the Ulster Unionist Council?
2. (a) To what extent does Document B show that Faulkner was 'pushed too far', as stated in Document A?
   (b) Which group listed in Document A had the victory in Document B? Explain your answer.
3. (a) Are both documents, A and B, primary sources? Explain your answer.
   (b) What difficulties did the journalists in Document B have in getting information and how would this affect their reliability?
4. How was Brian Faulkner's position as chief executive of the Northern Ireland Executive undermined?

SAMPLE QUESTION 3

Document A

Council of Ireland is Agreed
Dublin acknowledges status of North until majority expresses desire for change
By James Downey, Political Correspondent, in Sunningdale

After four days of talks, the Tripartite Conference of representatives of the Irish and British Governments and the Northern Ireland Executive-designate came to a successful conclusion here last night, with agreement on all the major issues before the conference.

There is to be a Council of Ireland with a Ministerial level consisting of seven each from North and South, a Secretariat and a Consultative Assembly, with 30 members each from the Dáil and the Northern Ireland Assembly... Britain is not to be represented on the council, but is to have safeguard to protect her financial and other interests. The Irish Government 'fully accepted and solemnly declared that there could be no change in the status of Northern Ireland until a majority of the people of Northern Ireland desired a change in that status.' In return, the British Government made a declaration that 'if in the future the majority of the people of Northern Ireland should indicate a wish to become part of a united Ireland, the British Government would support that wish.' This is regarded by Dublin as a substantial advance on the previous British position on consent to a united Ireland.

Source: *The Irish Times*, 10 December 1973.

Document B

'Sell-out' at talks say Extremists; Reaction to Announcement
From Walter Ellis and Fionnuala O'Connor

As the news of the Sunningdale settlement reached Northern Ireland last night, there were accusations from both extremes of the political divide of a sell-out. Mr William Craig, leader of the Vanguard Unionist Party, said he was 'utterly opposed' to the agreement.

Mr Harry West, leader of the Ulster Unionist Assembly Party (the unpledged Unionists), said that Mr Brian Faulkner would be in 'big trouble' when he returned home to sell the package to the loyalist community. He said that he would start immediate moves to have Mr Faulkner sacked as leader of the Unionist Party. Mr Faulkner had gone against Unionist policy in agreeing to a Council of Ireland having executive powers and not just being an advisory body.

Mr Michael Farrell, of the People's Democracy, said that the SDLP and the Dublin Government had conceded everything. He added that the South was becoming the 'third policeman of British rule in Ireland.'

Source: *The Irish Times*, 10 December 1973.

Document C

Ulster Unionist Council poster and slogan for the February 1974 general election.

Source: Publicity Department, Ulster Unionist Council.

1. (a) According to Document A, how many ministers would form part of the ministerial level of the Council of Ireland?
   (b) What was the proposed total number in the Consultative Assembly?
   (c) How did Harry West describe Brian Faulkner's position after the Sunningdale Agreement, according to Document B?
   (d) What did Michael Farrell accuse the SDLP and the Dublin government of doing?
   (e) What is the message of the poster in Document C?
2. (a) What aspect of the Agreement in Document A did Harry West say was against Unionist Party policy?

(b) Does the poster in Document C agree with the views of Michael Farrell in Document B?

3. (a) Is the heading of the story in Document B matched by the contents of the report?

   (b) How successful is the poster (Document C) in getting its message across?

4. To what extent was Brian Faulkner 'pushed further than he should have been' by the Sunningdale Agreement?

SAMPLE QUESTION 4

Document A

Loyalists removed by RUC as Assembly sits
Meeting gets down to business after protestors locked out
By Conor O'Clery, Our Northern Editor

As expected, the first meeting of the Northern Ireland Assembly since the Executive was formed began yesterday afternoon with scenes of uproar and pandemonium. Many loyalists, including the Rev. Ian Paisley, were carried struggling from the chamber by dozens of policemen after incredible scenes on the floor of the House.

The Assembly, the public gallery and the press gallery were packed for the opening of the Assembly at 2.30 p.m., and it was clear immediately that there was trouble in the air... Dr Paisley, hair falling over his eyes, helped his colleagues to grab three chairs to use them as makeshift barricades...to prevent the removal of the loyalists including himself... Dozens of members of the RUC then advanced into the chamber and began bodily carrying out the protestors. Mr Beattie was the first to go. Mr McQuade was carried out yelling 'You're murdering me.' Then Dr Paisley, carried lengthways by at least eight RUC men.

However, with 18 disaffected loyalists safely locked outside the Stormont building after an hour of disturbances, the remaining 60 or so Assembly members were able to conduct one-and-a-half hours of peaceful debate.

Source: *The Irish Times*, 23 January 1974.

Document B

An extract from a biography of Rev. Ian Paisley on how his popularity increased.

It was the first evidence of what later became an accepted part of Unionist wisdom – that Paisley's ruthlessness gains him more advantage than anyone else when he joins in coalition with other Loyalists. Paisley made the most gains when the Loyalists escalated their opposition inside and outside the Assembly following agreement in November to set up the Executive and to take office the following 1 January.

In the Assembly the Loyalists' tactics were to disrupt debates with noisy protests and DUP members were in the fore each time. The protests were intensified after the Sunningdale negotiations. ... The protests earned Paisley and the DUP considerable publicity and the admiration of militants outside. ... Paisley had one major advantage over Craig and West. He was much more forceful and articulate on TV and radio and as a result the media sought him out for comment. This helped to enhance the impression that he was leading the Loyalists' campaign...

Source: Ed Moloney and Andy Pollack, *Paisley*, Poolbeg Press, Dublin, 1986.

1. (a) When did the scenes of uproar and pandemonium occur, according to Document A?
   (b) Who grabbed the three chairs to use as a makeshift barricade?
   (c) How many loyalists were locked out of the Assembly?
   (d) What were the loyalists' tactics in the Assembly, according to Document B?
   (e) What advantage did Paisley have over Craig and West?
2. (a) What actions in Document A might earn 'Paisley and the DUP considerable publicity and the admiration of militants outside' (Document B)?
   (b) How would the actions of Document A 'disrupt debates' (Document B)?
3. (a) Is there evidence of bias in Document A? Explain your answer.
   (b) Which document is more factual and which is more analytical? Explain your answer.
4. What part did Rev. Ian Paisley play in relation to the Sunningdale Agreement and the downfall of the power-sharing executive?

SAMPLE QUESTION 5

Document A

Strike Issue Breaks Up NI Executive
Unionists resign after demand for mediation is refused by Rees

By Conor O'Clery, Northern Editor

The five-month-old Northern Ireland Executive, formed by Unionists, the SDLP and the Alliance Party during protracted negotiations with the British Government last autumn, broke up early yesterday afternoon. Northern Ireland now faces a return to an uncertain period of direct rule.

The Executive, which took office on January 1st, collapsed because of deep divisions between Unionist and SDLP Ministers over whether to negotiate with the organisers of the loyalist anti-Sunningdale strike, which, after 14 days, had brought the North to the verge of anarchy.

Mr Faulkner said it was apparent to them, from the extent of the support for the strike, that the degree of consent needed to sustain the Executive did not at present exist. SDLP Ministers in the Executive had refused earlier to support a Unionist and Alliance decision to recommend the commencement of a dialogue with the strikers.

Northern Ireland has now in effect come under de facto direct rule, with the British Government resuming the powers it held during the period April 1972 to December 1973.

Source: *The Irish Times*, 29 May 1974.

Document B

Editorial comment in The Irish Times *the day after the power-sharing executive fell.*

God Save Ulster!

A great experiment has ended; but there will be another day... The Loyalists have been on the winning side down the decades. They suffered some reverses in recent years. Now, in their eyes, this lost ground is being made good by the collapse of the Executive.

Their cause was a dreadful one. For the strike by the Ulster Workers' Council may have been claimed to be about a new election, about this, that or the other thing. It was, in fact, aimed at power-sharing, i.e. it was aimed against a fair deal for Catholics.

The strike was spectacularly successful for several reasons, but primarily because all the important jobs in the essential industries were held by Loyalists.

The boneless Harold Wilson let this strike go so far that he was helpless to stop it when at last he was provoked. The great moderate mass of Protestant Unionists of which so much has been heard did nothing about it. The Protestant Churches sounded no clarion call to remind their faithful of basic principles of fairness.

Source: *The Irish Times*, 29 May 1974.

1. (a) When did the power-sharing executive begin and end, according to Document A?
   (b) Why did the executive collapse, according to Document A?
   (c) What will happen under direct rule, according to Document A?
   (d) How have the loyalists made up 'lost ground', according to Document B?
   (e) Give one reason for the success of the strike, according to Document B.
2. (a) How does Document A differ from Document B on the reasons for the downfall of the executive?
   (b) Do Documents A and B agree on the reasons for the strike?
3. (a) Is Document A a balanced and fair account? Support your answer with evidence from the document.
   (b) Whose side does the writer of Document B favour?
4. What caused the collapse of the power-sharing executive in Northern Ireland?

OTHER CONTEXTUAL QUESTIONS ON THE SUNNINGDALE AGREEMENT AND THE POWER-SHARING EXECUTIVE, 1973–74

1. What part did the government of the Irish Republic play in the negotiations which led to the Sunningdale Agreement?
2. What was the significance of the Sunningdale Agreement and the power-sharing executive, 1973–74?
3. What was John Hume's contribution to the Sunningdale Agreement and the power-sharing executive?

CASE STUDY: THE COLERAINE UNIVERSITY CONTROVERSY

Answering Question 2 (Comparison) and Question 3 (Criticism) in the Documents Study

In answering Q2 and Q3, you should make use of information from both documents (or all, if there are three documents).

We can use **Sample Question 1 from the Coleraine University Controversy Case Study**.

Q2(a) asks, 'What criteria for an adequate site outlined in Document A are not fulfilled in Document B?'

In your answer, you can refer to the size of the site. Point out that the Lockwood Committee needs a site of 'about 300 acres' and 'much more' if they include agriculture. But Magee College in Document B has 'about 20 acres'. You can say that the Committee wants space for proposed activities, future growth and residential accommodation on a single site, but that Magee in Document B is already strained and shares science facilities with other colleges.

Q2(b) asks, 'How much smaller was Magee College (Document B) compared to the proposed second university (Document A)?'

In your answer, you can refer to the size of the site and the number of proposed students in the new university against the number of existing students in Magee.

Q3(a) asks, 'What are the limitations of these sources in analysing the reasons why the Lockwood Committee decided against Magee College as the site of the second university?'

In your answer, you are assessing the strengths and weaknesses of these sources and considering how you would find out the reasons for the decision. You can refer to these as published reasons – laying out the criteria helps to understand why they decided. But the sources don't give direct reasons as to why Magee was rejected – they are inferred. The sources don't give us information on the discussions of the Committee, such as the minutes of meetings. Neither do they give papers or reports prepared for the Committee or the pressure put on the Committee by others, often through informal discussion outside the meetings. You can then make your judgment on 'the limitations of these sources'.

Q3(b) asks, 'Is there evidence of bias in the writing of these sources? Explain your answer.'

This question asks you to explain your answer. But even if it did not, you should always explain your answer – that is what the marks are given for. You could begin by briefly defining 'bias', then examine both documents for the language of bias. You will note that Document A is laying out criteria in a straightforward manner and Document B is giving a factual description of the existing conditions in Magee College, so there is very little evidence of bias. But you can also point out that the bias may be in the selection of the criteria to the exclusion of others. You can't know if this selection is biased unless you have further information, such as the manner in which the Committee concluded its criteria, or whether the Committee excluded information in its description of Magee. This would mean further investigation or research. You can say you are using two documents from the one source – the Lockwood Report – and that you would need to have other sources to come to a final judgment.

In summary, in answering Q2 and Q3 of the documents study, use evidence from both documents as well as evidence about the documents given in the caption(s) of the documents.

> **The answers to Q4 (Contextualisation) in the documents-based Case Studies should be about two pages long.**
> **You should use the essay plans which follow to practise writing paragraphs or full answers.**

What were the conclusions of the Lockwood Committee in relation to a second university for Northern Ireland?

Intro: Robbins Report provided comprehensive survey of higher education in Britain – need for the same in NI; Lockwood Committee set up by Stormont government; members from England and NI – to report on higher education in Northern Ireland, especially on whether there should be a second university; presentations made to committee by Derry, Coleraine and Armagh for site of second university; reported after a year – estimated need for 12,000 to 13,000 student places in NI by 1980.

1. Need for second university: Economic development of North – need for scientists, technologists, teachers; structural change in economy – decline of shipbuilding, linen – need for newer industries; rejected the expansion of Queen's University – Queen's themselves opposed to it – site too small – close to houses – expensive to buy land; move away from Belfast; wanted a new type of university – based on agriculture and biological sciences, Education Centre for teacher education.

2. Arguments for Coleraine: Why? Fit criteria – could get site there; suitable for marine biology studies; suitable accommodation for students – use of summer boarding houses – so no need for expensive student accommodation; counter the pull of Belfast; timing – need to develop quickly; different background to Queen's – different kind of university to Queen's; not a competitor with Belfast for urban industry so therefore would not have faculties/departments which would weaken Queen's; could attract first-rate staff to nice area – housing accommodation to rent short term, easy to build longer term; convenient to Belfast and Aldergrove airport; support of local council.

3. Rejected Derry and Armagh: Could get a suitable site but shortage of private accommodation so need for expensive student accommodation: Derry opposition from officials in Ministry of Commerce – said Derry was too remote, Derry never lost 'the siege mentality' – local sectarian tension; inadequacy of Magee – site too small – governing structure poor – no academic representation on trustees who ran College – (others said seven 'faceless men' from Londonderry Unionist Association said to be opposed to siting of Derry); Armagh – could get site but poor housing situation; population too small to service a university; too close to Belfast – would not develop independently; opposed to Craigavon because the city was only in planning stages.

4. What to do with Magee: Lockwood Committee recommended closing it – buildings and site not regarded as a nucleus for a new university – not suitable for expansion; would affect the success of new university; would only be a drain on resources needed for the new university; suitable for non-university type course or residential adult education

5. Ulster College: Amalgamation of Belfast College of Technology, Domestic Science and Art – to develop technical education – non-university qualifications.

Conclusion: Political aspects of decision not taken into account by Lockwood – led to University for Derry Campaign; reinforced feeling of neglect in Derry – contributed to nationalist grievances; Stormont government go ahead with Lockwood proposals except does not close Magee College. Magee became a constituent college of the New University – later Coleraine University merged in October 1984 with Jordanstown Polytechnic, Magee College in Derry and Belfast Art College to form the University of Ulster.

What were the arguments for and against the siting of the new university in Coleraine?

Intro: Lockwood Committee on higher education; decided on second university; also decided on site of it – recommended Coleraine; University for Derry Committee – joint unionist–nationalist committee – organised against decision.

1. Arguments for Coleraine: Could get site there; suitable for marine biology studies; suitable accommodation – use of summer boarding houses – so no need for expensive student accommodation; counter the pull of Belfast; timing – need to develop quickly; different background to Queen's – different kind of university to Queen's; not a competitor with Belfast for urban industry so therefore would not have facilities which would weaken Queen's; could attract first-rate staff to nice area – housing accommodation to rent short term, easy to build longer term; convenient to Belfast and Aldergrove airport; support of local council. Arguments against Coleraine: no cultural amenities, also too small to sustain a university.

2. Arguments against Derry and Armagh – possible alternative sites: Derry could get a suitable site but shortage of private accommodation so need for expensive student accommodation; Derry opposition from officials in Ministry of Commerce – said Derry was too remote, Derry never lost 'the siege mentality' – local sectarian tension; inadequacy of Magee – site too small – governing structure poor – no academic representation on trustees who ran college – (others said seven 'faceless men' from Londonderry Unionist Association said to be opposed to siting of Derry); Armagh – could get site but poor housing situation; population too small to service a university; too close to Belfast – would not develop independently; opposed to Craigavon because the city was only in planning stages.

3. Case for Derry: Magee College could be basis for new university – in existence since mid-19th century; if Magee not suitable, other sites could be used in Derry; Derry had historic claims to be 'The Site'; Derry was the North's second city – only one large enough to sustain a university; need to build up Derry and north-west as a counterbalance to Belfast – attract more industry; brain drain from Derry if there is no university; university in Derry could increase cross-border co-operation with Donegal; need to treat nationalist community fairly.

Conclusion: Nationalists (and Derry unionists) said decision to site in Coleraine was more neglect of Derry; nationalists said it was deliberate – build up unionist areas to maintain unionist power – led to further controversy.

Why was there controversy over the selection of Coleraine as the site for a second university in Northern Ireland?

Intro: Lockwood Committee on higher education; decided on a second university; but also decided on site of it – recommended Coleraine.

1. Case against Coleraine: Size of town, nationalists said it was selected because it was majority Protestant.

2. Case for Derry: Magee College could be basis for new university – in existence since mid-19th century; if Magee not suitable other sites could be used in Derry; Derry had historic claims to be 'The Site'; Lockwood Committee's terms of reference did not include the question of the site; Derry was the North's second city – only one large enough to sustain a university; need to build up Derry and north-west as a counterbalance to Belfast – attract more industry; need to treat nationalist community fairly.

3. Nationalist feeling: Angry at decision to site university in Coleraine – said unionists did not want to develop Derry because of nationalist majority – would lose the few unionist seats they held – instead they would develop unionist Belfast–Coleraine–Portadown triangle and cause migration from west to east NI, scattering the nationalist minority – enable unionists to get a stronger grip on power (J. Hume); neglect of second city – Mathew Report – proposal for new city – Craigavon – Armagh; also ending of one of the rail links from Derry to Belfast; higher unemployment in Derry; feeling of betrayal, 'passing over' Derry; Lockwood also said that if North needed a third university in the future, Armagh would be suitable – issue of 'faceless, nameless men' from Londonderry Unionist Association – proof of unionist conspiracy for nationalists.

4. Campaign: University for Derry Committee started when rumours spread about Coleraine; Derry unionists and nationalists came together; cross-section of professional and business men; organised mass rally in Derry before publication of Lockwood Report; after publication, organise motorcade to Stormont – 2,000 cars, led by unionist mayor and Nationalist MP; gave documents to Prime Minister Terence O'Neill, showing sites in Derry.

Conclusion: Lockwood Committee recommended closure of Magee College but unionist government did not sanction that – fear of Derry protests; University for Derry Committee failed to change mind of unionist government on Coleraine, decision in favour of Coleraine contributed to nationalist feeling of discrimination.

What part was played by Terence O'Neill and/or John Hume in the Coleraine University controversy?

Intro: Lockwood Committee on higher education; decide on second university; also decided on site of it – recommended Coleraine.

1. O'Neill: Prime Minister, bringing in liberal reforms, trying to accommodate nationalists, Catholics; rejected Eddie McAteer's (nationalist MP for Derry) proposal for 'Orange and Green' talks on the university issue – instead appointed Lockwood Committee to report on higher education in NI.

2. Attitude to Lockwood: Discussion in Cabinet – opposed to closing Magee because of strength of political lobby – eventually got agreement of Cabinet not to close Magee – Magee became constituent college of New University – but backed Lockwood proposal for Coleraine – imposed a party whip on unionist MPs to pass Lockwood Report in Parliament, also made it a vote of confidence in his government – issue damaged O'Neill's reputation amongst nationalists.

3. John Hume: Teacher in local secondary school – interested in development of his community in Derry – founder of Campaign for Derry University when news that Coleraine was selected leaked out – Hume was chairman – meeting in Guildhall Derry of unionists and nationalists – speech by Hume emphasising unity of two communities – organised motorcade to Stormont to present views to Prime Minister O'Neill – Hume did not go.

4. Hume: Looked on university decision as proof of further 'isolation of the West' – spoke at Campaign for Democracy in Ulster (CDU) meeting in Fulham on issue – CDU dominated by Labour MPs – Hume saw university decision as part of unionist scheme to maintain power in NI by refusing to develop areas west of the Bann – keep development to Belfast–Coleraine–Portadown area – wanted MPs to use their influence with British government to reverse this trend.

Conclusion: Issue contributed to nationalist disenchantment with unionism – seen as further proof of discrimination – highlighted by Hume – contributed to origins of the Troubles.

CASE STUDY: THE APPRENTICE BOYS OF DERRY

What was the contribution of the Apprentice Boys of Derry to the celebration of religious and cultural identity amongst the city's unionist minority?

Intro: Apprentice Boys of Derry Club founded in 1814 to commemorate Siege of Derry – siege by army of Catholic King James – closing of the gate by Apprentice Boys and relief of siege by ships – siege relieved after 105 days – not attached to Orange Order.

1. Apprentice Boys: Governing body = General Committee, representatives of eight parent clubs (and associated clubs) – mostly founded in 19th century – parent clubs named after heroes of the Siege and events associated with the siege, e.g. Apprentice Boys of Derry Club named after the 'Brave 13' – the Apprentice Boys who closed the gates of the city; No Surrender Club named after the slogan or watchword of the Siege; Campsie Club named after one of the Apprentice Boys – members must be of Reformed Protestant religion, will support the Throne, keep alive the memories of the Siege and attend celebrations.

2. Meaning of parades: To commemorate Siege and Protestant religion and culture; stress on cultural links with Britain; relief of Derry celebrated on 12 August, shutting of the gates on 18 December – celebrated because Siege guaranteed civil and religious liberty – after it, Britain on the road to parliamentary democracy.

3. Meaning of parades: Thanksgiving service at St Columb's (Anglican) Cathedral – cathedral featured in the Siege – firing of cannon, a replica of 'Roaring Meg', the Siege cannon – Crimson flag flown – also crimson collarettes worn by Apprentice Boys to commemorate flag flown during the Siege – visit to the four gates of the city – walk along the Walls of Derry – burning of effigy of Lundy (governor of city who wanted to negotiate a surrender) on 18 December – 'Maiden City' that refused to be broken.

4. Outside Derry: Branch clubs affiliated to parent clubs formed in other parts of NI – new members initiated within the Derry city walls, usually on 12 August or 18 December – Lord Brookeborough, Terence O'Neill, Brian Faulkner, Ian Paisley initiated as members – trains and buses bring members to main parades in Derry – local parades held in localities also – spreading of aims and ideas of Apprentice Boys.

5. Growth of parades: Growth of Apprentice Boys from 1940s to 1990s – 178 branches in 1971, over 200 in 1989 – increase in numbers visiting city for parades – about 1,000 new members initiated each year – 300th anniversary of Siege celebrated with widespread celebrations in city in conjunction with nationalist city council – why? Siege of Derry a powerful symbol for unionists and Protestants in NI – spread of 'Troubles' – unionists and Protestants see their political and cultural heritage under threat.

Conclusion: You can emphasise here how the symbol of the Siege is important in unionist and Protestant thinking because of the changing political situation since the 1960s.

Why were the activities of the Apprentice Boys a source of tension in Derry City?

Intro: Apprentice Boys of Derry commemorate the Siege of Derry – relief of city 12 August, shutting of the gates 18 December – flashpoints for riots – conflict with nationalists and Catholics.

1. Apprentice Boys: Members must be of Reformed Protestant religion, will support the Throne, keep alive the memories of the Siege and attend celebrations – celebrate Protestant religion and culture – Siege represents unity in adversity, no compromise, no surrender – danger of traitor inside – never trust the enemy – exclude them from power.

2. Catholic/nationalist view: See Siege as defeat of Catholic King James leading to Protestant Ascendancy – defeat of Catholics in Ireland – walk on Walls of City and burning of effigy of Lundy overlooking the Bogside; nationalists a majority in Derry but due to unionist gerrymandering, unionist control of city council – seen as part of their status as second-class citizens – parades seen as symbol of nationalist subordination, sectarian, triumphalist – reminder of dominance of unionism in Stormont.

3. Parades: Apprentice Boys said they have right to parade – parade 'traditional' – central to Protestant identity, sense of belonging – regarded civil rights parades as not traditional – should be banned – source of conflict/tension; 1968 – civil rights march for Derry – Apprentice Boys plan march on same route at same time – civil rights march banned, but went ahead – clash with police.

4. 12 August, 18 December: Added to tension already in NI in 1960s – August 1969 – build-up – should parade be banned? Danger of breakdown of law and order – Hume to London and Dublin – prayers in churches that there would be no trouble – warnings that people of Bogside would defend themselves – walk on walls, pennies thrown down – Bogside youths throw stones – attacked by RUC – led to Battle of the Bogside – British army brought in.

5. Parades banned: Banned in 1970 and 1971 – church services held; parade restricted to Waterside for next few years, next year allowed into walled city but not onto walls because it overlooked nationalist Bogside – walking on walls banned until 1995.

Conclusion: Conflict between unionists and nationalists cause of tension – parades were a spark which brought the two sides into conflict.

CASE STUDY: THE SUNNINGDALE AGREEMENT AND THE POWER-SHARING EXECUTIVE

What factors contributed to the formation of a power-sharing executive in Northern Ireland, 1973–74?

Intro: Fall of Stormont – failure of unionism – divisions in society, riots, British Army introduced, direct rule.

1. IRA and Loyalist violence: IRA campaign – deaths and bombings 1972 (highest death toll – 467 killed) and 1973 – direct rule did not break cycle of violence – British military strategy would not win – loyalist violence – rioting, sectarian murders, loyalist strike – political solution needed.

2. Role of Faulkner and unionists: Lost power in Stormont – wanted it back – prepared to accept power-sharing.

3. Nationalists: SDLP voice of (moderate) nationalism, victory in local elections, represented majority of nationalists – need to isolate the IRA – chance of getting power.

4. Whitelaw, Secretary of State: Ability to compromise, conciliatory – Darlington Conference on options for NI – showed extent of agreement and disagreement in NI – referendum on the Border March 1973 pleased unionists – Operation Motorman to take down barricades in Bogside and Belfast – more unionist goodwill.

5. White Paper: Constitutional Proposals for Northern Ireland – Assembly – domestic policy – power-sharing executive – parties from both communities – Irish dimension – trying to appease SDLP, not upset official unionists too much.

6. Assembly elections 1973: Unionists, SDLP, Alliance Party = 60 per cent of electorate; later agreed make-up of power-sharing executive – six unionists, four SDLP, one Alliance.

7. Sunningdale Conference: New government in southern Ireland – Garret FitzGerald won respect of Westminster politicians; Heath worked for agreement, loyalists not invited – agreement on Council of Ireland (Irish Dimension) – power-sharing executive took office on 1 Jan 1974.

Conclusion: Seemed a success – compromise for unionists and nationalists; but weakness was many unionists opposed (more than Faulkner unionists) – also paramilitaries opposed.

How was Brian Faulkner's position as chief executive of the Northern Ireland Executive undermined?

Intro: Chief executive of power-sharing executive – Constitutional Proposals and Sunningdale Agreement – unionists, SDLP and Alliance Party – but Assembly elections 1973 – majority of unionists against power-sharing and Council of Ireland.

1. Faulkner's situation: Ulster Unionist Council rejected Sunningdale Agreement – Faulkner resigned as leader of Unionist Party – split in official unionism – set up Faulkner Ulster Unionist Party against United Ulster Unionist Coalition (UUUC) – anti-power-sharing/Sunningdale Agreement – effect of Kevin Boland's constitutional challenge to Sunningdale Agreement in southern courts.

2. Anti-agreement unionists: Dislike of sharing power with nationalists – dislike of Council of Ireland – seen as conspiracy for United Ireland – argued that Executive was imposed by Britain – did not represent majority of NI electorate (Westminster election) – dislike of influence of SDLP in power-sharing executive – pushed Council of Ireland – said it meant more than it did – IRA violence made unionists more hardline.

3. February general election: Called by Heath, PM of Britain – bad timing for NI – no organisation by Faulkner – UUUC (West, Craig and Paisley) agreed pact on candidates in constituencies – ran campaign of 'Who runs Ulster?' – UUUC won all unionist seats (SDLP won other seat) – UUUC favoured federal UK, with regional government in NI – power-sharing doomed.

4. Labour Party in power: General election in Britain won by Labour Party – Wilson PM, Merlyn Rees as Secretary of State – often in London – not knowledgeable on Northern problems – Wilson's speech during UWC strike on 'thugs and bullies', 'spongers'.

5. Ulster Workers Council (UWC) strike: Vote in Assembly in favour of Sunningdale – general strike 14 May – UWC in key industries and two main power stations – UDA intimidate workers – British government advised by British army not to do so – did not want to interfere – said job for police – split in power-sharing executive over negotiating with strikers – Faulkner resigned – power-sharing executive collapsed.

6. Role of Paisley: Changed from integration with UK – Democratic Unionist Party (DUP) second largest unionist grouping in Assembly – Paisley, Craig and West sat on UWC co-ordination committee which ran strike – once strike got hold, Paisley organised world media – dominant role – proposed calling off strike after executive collapsed.

Conclusion: Firm action earlier might have stopped strike but would not save power-sharing executive.

To what extent was Brian Faulkner 'pushed further than he should have been' by the Sunningdale Agreement?

Intro: British government Constitutional Proposals – Assembly, power-sharing executive – negotiations in Sunningdale for Irish Dimension – Council of Ireland.

1. British government: Whitelaw gone – replaced by Frances Pym – knew little about NI – took small part in negotiations – mainly done by Heath, PM – interest of NI subordinate to Britain.

2. Sunningdale talks: Faulkner isolated at talks – no agreed power-sharing executive voice – unionists and SDLP have separate representations at talks – SDLP have backing of Irish government – Faulkner does not have backing of British government – Heath saw Faulkner as a reactionary representative of old unionism; Faulkner wanted support of Irish government for anti-terrorism – prepared to go along with 'a limited amount of nonsense' on the Council – pressed for deletion of Articles 2 and 3 of Irish Constitution – told it would have to go to referendum, and would be defeated – got on well with Cosgrave, common interest in horses; loyalists not invited.

- **SDLP:** Divisions at talks – Gerry Fitt and Paddy Devlin did not want to push partition issue – John Hume did – traditional nationalist – wanted real progress towards unification; had respect of Irish government and Heath – pushed for real executive powers for Council of Ireland.

- **Irish government:** Hume pressed Irish government – Council of Ireland originally a minor role in Constitutional Proposals – co-operation on transport, tourism, etc. – now Irish government favoured enhanced status for Council (the Irish Dimension) – why? Isolate IRA, help SDLP – British government persuaded of case; Conor Cruise O'Brien (Irish government minister) would settle for power-sharing, did not want a strong Council of Ireland – fear of unionist backlash – but had to follow Irish government policy agreed at Cabinet.

3. Agreement: After four days – two-tier Council of Ireland – fourteen ministers and sixty-member Consultative Assembly – decisions unanimous – on economic and social co-operation – no commitment by Irish government to remove Articles 2 and 3 (Southern claim on NI) from the Irish Constitution – eight functions for Council of Ireland agreed – originally thirteen proposed – Devlin demanded them reduced – he would not have his unionist friends 'hung from lampposts' when they returned to Belfast.

4. Post-Agreement actions of unionists and loyalists: Ulster Unionist Council rejected Sunningdale Agreement – Faulkner resigned as leader of Unionist Party – split in official unionism – set up Faulkner Ulster Unionist Party against United Ulster Unionist Coalition

(UUUC) – anti-power-sharing/Sunningdale Agreement; effect of Kevin Boland's constitutional challenge to Sunningdale Agreement in southern courts; February general election – result of – Faulkner isolated; UWC strike – success of.

Conclusion: You must decide whether or not Faulkner was pushed too far.

What part did Rev. Ian Paisley play in relation to the Sunningdale Agreement and the downfall of the power-sharing executive?

Intro: Constitutional Proposals and Sunningdale Agreement – victory for nationalists, defeat for unionists – Paisley favoured integration with Britain – not popular; opposed to Craig, leader of Vanguard Unionist Party – both fighting for control of loyalism (extreme unionism).

1. Opposed to Constitutional Proposals: Paisley did not want power-sharing and Council of Ireland – danger of Irish unity; Paisley and Craig made pact to fight 1973 Assembly elections – DUP gained one seat more than Vanguard; Paisley made gains when loyalists upset Assembly – disrupted debates, intensified after Sunningdale Agreement and operation of power-sharing executive; Paisley removed from Assembly by eight RUC – Protestant militants admired Paisley's actions – Paisley's advantage – articulate on TV and radio – called on for comments – gave impression he was leader of loyalists.

2. Save Ulster: Campaign in late 1973 to protest British refusal to invite extreme unionists to Sunningdale; Harry West and dissident unionists joined Paisley and DUP and Craig and Vanguard to form United Ulster Unionist Coalition (UUUC) to fight power-sharing and Council of Ireland.

3. February general election: Only one loyalist candidate in each constituency – disagreement over share of seats – West Unionists get seven, Craig got three, Paisley got two – Paisley secretly invited Official Unionist candidate to join DUP – he refused – Paisley's action nearly wrecked UUUC; result – victory for UUUC – all eleven unionist seats, Paisley increased his majority to 25,000 in North Antrim.

4. UWC strike: Paisley on UWC co-ordinating committee to run strike – had doubts about whether it would succeed, questioned its timing – date set for 14 May – day the Assembly would ratify Sunningdale Agreement; strike began slowly – Paisley in Toronto for funeral – some suggested he left because he thought strike would fail – saw it was working and came back – gave full backing to it – whipped up support, especially used media to present loyalists' case; Paisley proposed calling off strike when power-sharing executive fell – agreed by UWC.

Conclusion: Paisley took advantage of opposition to power-sharing and Council of Ireland – grew in popularity – benefited most from loyalist disruption.

What caused the collapse of the power-sharing executive in Northern Ireland?

Intro: Power-sharing executive – joint unionist–nationalist executive – Faulkner Unionists, SDLP and Alliance Party – collapsed in May 1974, five months after taking over.

1. Growth of unionist opposition: British Constitutional Proposals: opposition from unionists from beginning – Craig and Vanguard Party, Paisley and DUP, paramilitaries – opposed to power-sharing with nationalists, also to Irish Dimension because of fear of a united Ireland.

2. Faulkner loses unionist support: Assembly elections June 1973 – majority for Constitutional Proposals but 20 per cent for Paisley and Craig; power-sharing executive agreed in November 1973 but five Unionist Party MPs in Westminster withdraw support form Faulkner – disruption of Assembly meetings by loyalists – more disruption of Assembly after Sunningdale Agreement – Ulster Unionist Council rejected Sunningdale, Jan 1974 – Faulkner resigned as leader of Unionist Party – formed his own party – Ulster Unionist Party.

3. Sunningdale Agreement: Council of Ireland originally a minor role in Constitutional Proposals – co-operation on transport, tourism, etc. – enlarged powers for Council of Ireland at Sunningdale – more problems for Faulkner – more opposition from unionists; also Faulkner failed to get Irish government to agree to deletion of Articles 2 and 3 of Irish Constitution claiming control over NI – anti-Sunningdale parties come together as United Ulster Unionist Coalition (UUUC) – united front against Faulkner and power-sharing executive – effect of Kevin Boland's constitutional challenge to Sunningdale Agreement in southern courts.

4. February general election: Called by Heath, PM of Britain – bad timing for NI situation – no organisation by Faulkner – UUUC (West, Craig and Paisley) agreed pact on candidates in constituencies – ran campaign of 'Who runs Ulster?' – slogan 'Dublin Is Just a Sunningdale Away' – UUUC won all unionist seats (SDLP won other seat) – UUUC favoured federal UK, with regional government in NI – power-sharing doomed.

5. Labour Party in power: General election in Britain won by Labour Party – Wilson PM, Merlyn Rees as Secretary of State – often in London – not knowledgeable on Northern problems – Wilson's speech during UWC strike on 'thugs and bullies', 'spongers' – united loyalists.

6. Ulster Workers Council (UWC) strike: Vote in Assembly in favour of Sunningdale –

general strike – UWC in key industries and two main power stations – UDA intimidate workers – British government advised by British army not to do so – did not want to interfere – said job for police – split in power-sharing executive over negotiating with strikers – Faulkner resigned – power-sharing executive collapsed.

Conclusion: In your conclusion you should decide what were the key factors in the downfall of the power-sharing executive.

Section 3

ANSWERING QUESTIONS ON THE TOPICS

THE MARKING SCHEME

In Ordinary Level questions, paragraph and long answer questions are preceded by a **stimulus-driven unit** (extract, cartoon or photograph) with four or five short questions to be attempted (maximum 30 marks).

Paragraphs and long answers (also called longer paragraphs) are marked according to **core statements**. A core statement may be defined as one of the following:

* A **significant factual statement** that is relevant to the question asked.
* An **explanation, opinion or comment** that is relevant to the question asked.
* A **significant introductory or concluding statement** that is relevant to the question asked.

Each **completed core statement** is awarded **5 marks**.

An **incomplete core statement** at the end of an answer may merit **1–4 marks**.

Short paragraphs:

* In **short paragraph answers,** a maximum cumulative mark (CM) of 20 will be allowed for core statements and a maximum of 10 marks will be allowed for the examiner's overall evaluation (OE) of the answer.
* **Maximum of 20 marks for CM and maximum of 10 marks for OE.**

Long paragraphs:

* In **longer paragraph answers** (or long answers), a maximum cumulative mark of 30 will be allowed for core statements and a maximum of 10 marks will be allowed for the examiner's overall evaluation of the answer.
* **Maximum of 30 marks for CM and maximum of 10 marks for OE.**

Basically, the **CM** gives you marks for **the content or historical information** you use and the **OE** gives you marks for **how well you wrote it**, e.g. did you stick to the question, is your information in the correct order?

When you are writing your answers, don't try to guess how many core statements you have written. Let the examiners work that out. Instead, you must write more than enough in the short paragraphs and long paragraphs so that you get the maximum marks. You must balance this with the amount of time you can spend on each answer.

- Short paragraphs = 10 minutes.
- Longer paragraphs (long answers) = 15 minutes.

Cumulative Mark (CM)

This is the total mark awarded for core statements, subject to a maximum of 20 marks in short paragraph answers and a maximum of 30 marks in long answers.

Overall Evaluation (OE)

In awarding OE, the examiner will consider how well the answer responds to the heading or addresses the set question. The following grading table will apply:

- Excellent: 9–10 marks.
- Very good: 7–8 marks.
- Good: 5–6 marks.
- Fair: 3–4 marks.
- Poor: 0–2 marks.

PARAGRAPHS – SAMPLE ANSWERS

The Pursuit of Sovereignty and the Impact of Partition, 1912–49

Life in Ireland during the emergency

Ireland was neutral during the Second World War. The government, led by de Valera, declared a state of emergency. Imports were cut and there were shortages of goods and raw materials. The Ministry of Supplies was set up under Seán Lemass to get more supplies. Sugar, tea and fuel were rationed. There was less imported coal, so turf was used in trains. Journeys were slow. A train could take twelve hours to travel between Dublin and Cork. Irish Shipping was set up to buy and hire ships to bring supplies to Ireland. Merchant sailors risked their lives in submarine-infested waters to bring food to the country.

Compulsory tillage was introduced but yields were low because of a shortage of fertilizer. Industry was also short of raw materials, so many factory workers became unemployed. Living standards fell as prices rose and wages were kept down by government order. Thousands emigrated to Britain to work in the war industries or join the British army. Ireland experienced some bombing, such as in the North Strand in Dublin, when German planes killed twenty-seven people.

The United States and the World, 1945–89

Advances in space technology

The US government set up NASA (National Aeronautics and Space Administration) to organise American space exploration after the Russians sent the first rocket into space. The Russians also sent the first man into space – Yuri Gagarin – and this was followed soon after by the first American, Alan Shepard.

The US seemed to always be behind the Russians, so a big boost was given to American space technology when President Kennedy said the US would have a man on the moon before the end of the 1960s. The US used the Gemini Project to send two-man flights into space. They practised docking techniques and space walks. The US also surveyed the surface of the moon to select sites for landing.

Then they organised the Apollo mission. They used three-man spacecraft and orbited the moon. In 1969, three astronauts – Armstrong, Aldrin and Collins – lifted off from Cape Kennedy in Florida for the first manned flight to the moon. Armstrong and Aldrin landed on the moon while Collins orbited around the moon.

More flights followed and they used a moon buggy to get around the surface and collect rock samples for investigation. The Americans also sent spaceships to further planets, mainly trying to investigate signs of life. They also developed space stations with *Skylab*. The US also used a space shuttle – the first was called *Columbia* – which could be reused. Advances in space technology also helped weather forecasting and communications.

LONG ANSWERS – SAMPLE ANSWERS

The Pursuit of Sovereignty and the Impact of Partition, 1912–49

What was the role of Michael Collins in the Treaty negotiations, 1921?

De Valera insisted that Michael Collins become a delegate to the Treaty negotiations in London. Collins reluctantly agreed. He believed he would be more useful in Ireland if the talks broke down. Collins was one of the chief negotiators, along with Griffith and Barton.

Collins did not trust Erskine Childers, who was secretary to the delegation. He regarded him as a spy for de Valera.

Collins went with the Irish delegation to London in October 1921. They were given the title 'plenipotentiaries', which meant they had full power. But any agreement reached would have to be communicated to the Cabinet in Dublin before they signed it. At the start of the negotiations, the full delegations met each other. But as the talks progressed, sub-committees were formed. Collins played a key role in the sub-committees.

One of the problems was Ulster. Collins and Griffith agreed to a Boundary Commission to sort out the border between North and South. Collins believed that a Commission would move predominantly nationalist areas such as Fermanagh, Tyrone, South Armagh and Derry city out of Northern Ireland. He also hoped that the threat of such a Commission would force Craig to compromise on the issue of recognising an all-Ireland parliament. Collins and the other delegates returned to Dublin to report to the Cabinet in early December. Some members of the Cabinet disagreed with Collins and the delegates. When they returned to London, they proposed de Valera's idea of external association, but the British rejected it and the talks broke down. Collins was under considerable pressure. He was keenly aware of how ill-equipped the IRA was to resume a war against superior British forces. He also believed that the British had gone as far as they could go in the negotiations.

When Lloyd George, the British prime minister, gave the delegates an ultimatum, Griffith agreed to sign first, then Collins agreed. Collins believed that he had signed his own death warrant. But he also believed that the Treaty was a stepping stone to full Irish independence.

Dictatorship and Democracy in Europe, 1920–45

How did Joseph Goebbels use propaganda to support the Nazi state?
When Hitler became chancellor of Germany in 1933, he appointed Goebbels as Minister of Enlightenment and Propaganda. Goebbels was very loyal to Hitler and he used all means of propaganda to ensure Nazi control of the German state. Goebbels believed that if you tell a big lie often enough, people will believe you.

Goebbels divided the Ministry of Propaganda into sections to control press, radio and cinema. Newspapers could only print what Goebbels wanted. He held a daily press conference for editors and they were instructed on what view they should take on various issues. Jewish editors were fired and anti-Nazi newspapers were closed. He also organised a book burning to destroy anti-Nazi books.

Goebbels said radio was very important for controlling the masses of people. He wanted everyone to buy a People's Radio which could only broadcast Nazi stations. By 1939 there were four times more radios in Germany than in 1933. He also set up loudspeakers in the streets to broadcast Hitler's speeches.

Goebbels also used cinema for propaganda. He used newsreels to boast about Hitler's achievements. Movies were used to spread Nazi ideas about the Jews (anti-Semitism). One of those movies was called *The Eternal Jew*.

Goebbels also used huge crowds at marches, parades and torchlight processions to give an impression of Nazi strength. Goebbels used the Olympic Games in Berlin in 1936 as a great propaganda event for Nazi Germany. The organisation of the event impressed foreigners. Goebbels was also involved in the Nuremberg Rallies, the huge rallies held every year for all branches of the Nazi organisation. These rallies ensured that Nazi members went back to their hometowns to spread Nazi propaganda.

Goebbels encouraged the cult of the leader, Hitler. He used slogans such as *'Ein Reich, Ein Volk, Ein Führer'* ('One Country, One People, One Leader') and he put up posters and photographs of Hitler in many places. Goebbels also knew that education was important for propaganda. The Nazis made sure that schoolbooks and lessons followed their ideas. Children were taught to love their Führer and Hitler was often photographed with children. On Hitler's birthday, they put flowers beside his photograph at home and in school. Children were brainwashed by Nazi ideas.

During the Second World War, Goebbels had to maintain morale in Germany. This was easy when Germany was winning the war by defeating France and attacking Russia. But after the Battle of Stalingrad, Goebbels had to use propaganda to keep up the spirit of the people even though they were losing the war.

The United States and the World, 1945–89

Why did the United States become so heavily involved in Vietnam in the 1960s?
The US increased their involvement in Vietnam in the 1960s because they looked on the conflict there as a Cold War conflict. They believed that by helping the South Vietnamese government, they were containing communism. The South Vietnamese government was fighting against the Viet Cong, who were South Vietnamese communists backed by the North Vietnamese communist government.

President Kennedy of America also believed in the domino theory – that if South Vietnam fell to the communists, all other countries around them would also fall. President Kennedy did not want to send in US troops, but he increased the number of 'advisers' to

23,000. Their job was to train the South Vietnamese army to fight the Viet Cong guerrillas, but they were gradually brought into the fighting themselves.

President Johnson also increased the number of US 'advisers'. He felt that US credibility was at stake – if the US did not stand up for their ally, South Vietnam, nobody would trust them in the future. Some of Johnson's Cabinet believed that a military solution was the only one for Vietnam. Once the war expanded, President Johnson did not want to be the first president to lose a war.

But limited US help was not working. President Johnson realised that the South Vietnamese government was not strong enough to stop the Viet Cong. He believed he had to either withdraw from Vietnam or else bring in much greater numbers of US troops.

When North Vietnamese boats fired on two US warships in the Gulf of Tonkin in 1964, President Johnson used this as an excuse to send in more US troops. Congress passed the Tonkin Resolution, which gave the president power to wage war. Johnson increased the number of US troops to half a million by 1967. He also gave the go-ahead for air bombing of North Vietnam to stop them helping the Viet Cong.

The US was fighting a guerrilla war. The Viet Cong used the forests of South Vietnam and the support of the villages. The US used search and destroy missions, but they did not work. They also used napalm and chemicals on the forests to hunt out the enemy. They found it very difficult to defeat the enemy – by the end of 1968, the US had suffered 200,000 casualties, including 30,000 dead. The military leaders believed that only the use of more and more troops would lead to victory. They still believed they were winning the war until the Tet Offensive in 1968.

Answering Higher Level Questions

ESSAY WRITING IN THE RESEARCH STUDY AND TOPICS

The skills of essay writing are needed in the Extended Essay in the Research Study, and they form the basis of the remaining questions on the Topics that will be examined in the final examination.

In the final examination in June:

- You will have a choice of **one question** out of **four** in each of the three Topics.
- Each of the essays is worth **100 marks**.

THE MARKING SCHEME

You are asked to respond to a **historical question**. Your answers will be marked under two headings:

- **Cumulative mark** (CM) for **historical content** that is **accurate** and **relevant** to the question as asked. Maximum CM = **60 marks**.
- **Overall evaluation** (OE) for the **quality** of the answer as a whole in the context of the set question. Maximum OE = **40 marks**.

Your answer is marked in **paragraphs or paragraph equivalents**. A paragraph or paragraph equivalent is:

- A relevant introduction, giving the background situation and/or defining the terms and explaining the approach.
- An episode, phase or stage in a sequence of events.
- An aspect of a topic/issue, with supporting factual references.
- A point in an argument or discussion, with supporting factual references.
- An explanation of a concept or term, with supporting factual references.
- A number of significant, relevant statements of fact, explanation or comment which, although not connected or related, can be taken together and assessed as a paragraph equivalent.
- A good concluding paragraph or summation that is not mere repetition. (Summation which is mere repetition = max. 4 marks.)

The examiner will award marks to each paragraph or paragraph equivalent as follows (brackets are used to designate a paragraph or paragraph equivalent):

Cumulative mark (CM) (maximum = 60 marks):

• **Excellent: 11–12 marks.**	Outstanding piece of analysis, exposition or commentary. Clearly expressed, accurate and substantial information.
• **Very good: 8–10 marks.**	Very good material, accurately and clearly expressed.
• **Good: 6–7 marks.**	Worthwhile information, reasonably well expressed.

• **Fair: 3–5 marks.**	Limited information/barely stated.
• **Poor: 0–2 marks.**	Trivial/irrelevant/grave errors.

Note: Where individual questions have **two** elements, students are usually given a maximum CM = 50 if they refer to only **one** of those elements.

Example

The question 'To what extent did Stalin transform the society and economy of the Soviet Union?' (LC Higher Level 2006) has **two** elements in it – **society** and **economy**. If you answered this question and referred to only economy and did not mention society, then the maximum cumulative mark you could get is 50. However, you do not need to refer to both elements equally – an answer which deals mostly with the Soviet economy and only a little with Soviet society will be entitled to a maximum CM of 60 if it has enough historical content.

Overall evaluation (OE) (maximum = 40 marks):

• **Excellent: 34–40 marks.**	Excellent in its treatment of the set question.
• **Very good: 28–33 marks.**	Very good – but not excellent – in its treatment of the set question, i.e. accurate and substantial.
• **Good: 22–27 marks.**	Good standard treatment of the set question.
• **Fair: 16–21 marks.**	Fair attempt at the set question but has identifiable defects, e.g. incomplete coverage, irrelevant data, factual inaccuracies.
• **Weak: 10–15 marks.**	Poor in that it fails to answer the question as set, but has some merit.
• **Very weak: 0–9 marks.**	Very poor answer which at best offers only scraps of information.

In awarding the OE, the examiner will evaluate the quality of the answer, taking into account the following, as appropriate:

• To what extent has the candidate shown the ability to analyse the issues involved in the question asked (i.e. more than mere narrative)?

• To what extent has the candidate marshalled the relevant evidence to support his/her analysis?

- To what extent has the candidate shown the ability to argue a case and to reach conclusions (i.e. to answer the question as asked)?

THE ESSAY STRUCTURE

An essay is an **argument**, **a point of view** and/or **a line of reasoning** supported by historical evidence.

The essay is divided into an **introduction**, **paragraphs** and a **conclusion**.

In an introduction, you can:
- Show understanding of the question.
- Set the essay in context.
- Provide background information.
- Define terms, if necessary.
- Link to the first paragraph/rest of the essay

In paragraphs:
- Use **one** main theme or point.
- Begin with topic or linking sentence to state the main idea of the paragraph.
- Develop the argument of the essay using historical information.
- Make evidence relevant to the title of the essay.
- Use linking phrases or words (see p. 128).
- Use concluding or link sentence to wrap up paragraph, by linking the paragraph to the essay title.

In the conclusion:
- Draw together the main points.
- Come to a final conclusion.
- Set the essay topic in a broader context by briefly linking to other developments.
- Use new information; don't be repetitive.

It is important to understand what is being asked in each question.

Examples of wordings of essay-style questions:
- Why did…
- Why…/explain why…

- What were the factors...
- What were the aims and achievements...
- What changes...
- For what reasons...
- To what extent...
- How important/significant/influential was...
- What was the importance of.../what was the significance of ...
- What was the impact of...
- What impact had...
- What part did...
- What was the importance of...
- Which had the greater impact...
- How successful was...
- How extensive was...
- What role did...
- Do you consider...
- How true is (this statement)...
- How did (something) develop...
- What developments took place...
- What contribution did...
- What factors contributed to...
- What were the arguments for and against...
- How do you account for...
- In what ways were...
- ...and/or...
- ...one or more...

Example: Developing an Essay Structure

We will now use an example to develop an essay structure and paragraphs.

- The *title* of the essay is: '*How* did Hitler and the Nazis *consolidate power* and create a *totalitarian dictatorship* after coming to power in 1933?'
- Analyse the title and *underline* the key words.
- **What is the theme of the essay?** – Hitler and the Nazis in power.
- **What is being asked?** – How did they consolidate their power and create a totalitarian dictatorship?

- *Plan the structure of the essay* with *one main theme or topic* for the *introduction*, for each of about *five or six paragraphs* and a *conclusion* (about seven to eight paragraphs in total).

Note: Each paragraph is marked out of 12, so it is better to have more than five paragraphs (5 x 12 = maximum CM 60) because many paragraphs will not achieve the full 12 marks.

An essay plan:

- **Homework essay:** Having consulted your textbook and notes, develop a simple essay plan using one heading for each paragraph.
- **Exam essay:** You have about 41 minutes to write an essay in the examination (Higher Level), so use three to five minutes to develop the essay plan.
- **Keep it simple: Don't waste time writing out long essay plans in the exam – put the information into your essay instead.**

This is an essay plan for the example here:
How did Hitler and the Nazis *consolidate power* and create a *totalitarian dictatorship* after coming to power in 1933?'

Introduction:
- Hitler's rise to power – brief, condensed.

Paragraphs:
- General election and policy of co-ordination.
- SA and Night of Long Knives.
- Propaganda, including cult of personality.
- Police state and terror.
- Youth.

Conclusion:
- Extending totalitarian control through economy, army, churches, Jews, war.

Note: There is a wide range of information available for the topic of this question, much more than you need for the essay. Thus the main problem is trying to condense the information so that you finish the essay in time.

SAMPLE PARAGRAPHS

Sample introduction based on background of Hitler's rise to power and linking with establishment of totalitarianism*

*See p. 159 for the full essay.

> In January 1933, President Hindenburg appointed Hitler chancellor of Germany. His rise to power had been rapid. Hitler and the Nazis had only twelve seats in the Reichstag in 1928, but by 1932 they were the largest party in Germany. The Great Depression, the weaknesses of the Weimar Republic, Hitler's policies and propaganda and the violence of the SA and SS all contributed to the increased support for the Nazis. However, Hitler's intention was always to create a totalitarian dictatorship where he and his party would control all aspects of life, from the actions of people to their thoughts. He ensured this by taking over the state and using the power of the state to control other aspects of the political, economic and social life of Germany.

Filling in background

Use of historical information

Condensing causes

Defining term

Linking with later paragraphs

Two different paragraphs based on the same main theme of general election and co-ordination

> Once appointed chancellor, Hitler quickly established a dictatorship. In March 1933, he used the resources of the state to fight the general election which he called. Four hundred thousand SA were enlisted in the police and they used legal terror against communists and others. Hitler warned against the communist threat when a Dutch communist set fire to the Reichstag building. In the election, the Nazis increased their seats to 288 and, with the help of the nationalists, they passed the Enabling Act, which gave Hitler power to rule by decree. Hitler and the Nazis were able to use this power in a policy of co-ordination to ban other political parties, to abolish trade unions and to bring

Topic or link sentence back to title; stating main theme of paragraph; use of connecting words

Historical information in body of paragraph in support of main theme – establish a dictatorship the press under Nazi control. Within a short time, Hitler had brought the Weimar democracy to an end and established dictatorship.

> Concluding or link sentence at end, wrapping up main theme or point of paragraph

A second sample paragraph based on the main theme of general election and co-ordination, showing how students can draw on the same information to write two different paragraphs on the same main theme.

> Topic or link sentence back to title; stating main theme of paragraph; use of connecting words

Hitler became chancellor largely through legal means, but he quickly used the power of the state to establish a dictatorship. In the general election of March 1933, he used the SA as a police force against the communists. He and the Nazis increased their seats in the election. With the help of the nationalists, the Nazis passed the Enabling Law, which allowed Hitler to rule by decree. He now used this power in a policy of co-ordination which destroyed groups opposed to the Nazis. He outlawed the communists and the Social Democrats, brought the press under control and replaced trade unions with the German Labour Front. He also abolished State parliament and replaced them with Nazi governors. Within a short time, Hitler and the Nazis had established a dictatorship.

> Historical information in body of paragraph in support of main theme – establish a dictatorship

> Concluding or link sentence at end, wrapping up main theme or point of paragraph

Sample conclusion (after paragraphs on SA and Night of Long Knives; propaganda, including cult of personality; police state and terror; youth)

Hitler tightened his totalitarian control of Germany in other ways. With the death of Hindenburg in 1934, he made himself Führer and imposed an oath of loyalty on the German army. His Four Year Plan ensured a tighter grip by the Nazis on the German economy. He pressurised the

> Topic or link sentence

> No repetition

churches into acknowledging his leadership, though he had greater success with the Protestant churches than with the Catholic Church. He imposed the Nuremberg Laws on Jews and half of them emigrated by 1939. His success in foreign policy and his early victories in the Second World War bolstered support for him and the Nazis. But it also led to his downfall. Ultimately, it was Hitler's defeat in the war which ← ended his totalitarian dictatorship.

Concluding sentence

HOW WILL YOU GO ABOUT REVISION?

- **Prepare notes** on various areas of each topic you are studying, e.g. Dictatorship and Democracy (Mussolini, Hitler, Lenin and Stalin, Case Studies, etc). Maybe your class notes will do, or use revision guides for the Leaving Certificate. Add on where you think necessary.

- Compile a **list of questions** – begin with the most recent Leaving Cert exam questions and organise the questions **according to topics,** e.g. keep questions on Hitler together.

Example:

- What were the main characteristics of the Nazi state in Germany between 1933 and 1939? (LC 2007)

- During the inter-war period, what conditions in Europe contributed to the growth of fascist regimes? (LC 2006)

- **Sample (SEC):** To what extent did Germany's social and economic problems lead to the rise of Hitler and the Nazis?

- Add on more questions from **your textbook** or **exam papers.**

- Use **sample questions:** Select a topic, e.g. Hitler, then use the sample questions to look at the topic **from different angles or aspects** – his rise to power, when he got into power, his foreign policy, his treatment of the Jews, relations with the Christian churches, World War II, etc.

- Use your **notes** to write up some **essays** or make **essay plans.**

- Sometimes it helps to **work with a friend** to make essay plans.

Summary of guidelines on essay-writing:

- **Read** the question **carefully**.
- **Analyse the wording** of the question – what is the question asking? Underline the key words.
- Undertake preparatory **reading** and **note-taking** (if you are planning a homework essay).
- **Plan the structure** of the essay – **brainstorming** session to select **main themes or points.**
- List headings (main themes) for each paragraph or draw a spider diagram to lay out the structure of the essay.
- Write with a **clear style**.
- Use **short, simple words** rather than complicated ones.
- Don't use slang.
- Use **active verbs** rather than passive, e.g. 'Hitler ordered the assassination of Rohm' rather than 'The assassination of Rohm was ordered by Hitler.'
- Keep the **sentences short** and **vary the length** of the sentences.
- Write paragraphs of twelve to fifteen lines (this depends on the size of your handwriting).
- Begin paragraphs with a **topic or link** sentence.
- Conclude paragraphs with a **concluding** or **wrapping up sentence**.
- Make use of **connecting words or phrases** (connectives) within paragraphs and linking paragraphs (see below).
- Use **evidence or historical information** to support the main idea of each paragraph.
- In the exam, **answer all the questions you are asked** and **keep to the time allotted**.

Examples of Connecting Words or Phrases

Use connecting words and phrases to allow the essay to flow by linking information within and between paragraphs.

but, and, also, although, next, yet, as a result, however, likewise, similarly, in contrast, therefore, for example, it follows, instead, later, finally

- **Total time available = 2 hours 50 minutes.**
- **Higher Level:** Approximately **41 minutes** per question.
  (This is allowing 45 minutes for the documents-study question.)
- **Ordinary Level:** Paragraphs = 10 minutes. Long answers = 15 minutes.

REVISING THE CASE STUDIES

In studying for your exam, you should ensure that you revise the Case Studies in each topic because questions can be asked on these. The Case Studies play an important part in the Topics – you should know each Case Study, but **you should link them to other relevant parts of the Topic and Key Personalities.** Below are frameworks for studying each of the Case Studies, related Elements and Key Personalities.

Note that frameworks for the Case Studies on the Topic 'The United States and the World, 1945–89' appear on pp. 32–33 and 'Politics and Society in Northern Ireland, 1949–93' on pp. 74–75.

Topic: Movements for Political and Social Reform, 1870–1914

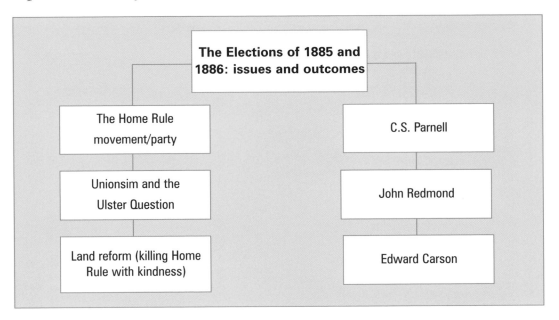

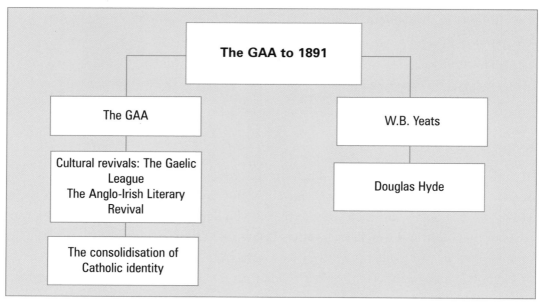

The GAA to 1891

The GAA

Cultural revivals: The Gaelic League
The Anglo-Irish Literary Revival

The consolidisation of Catholic identity

W.B. Yeats

Douglas Hyde

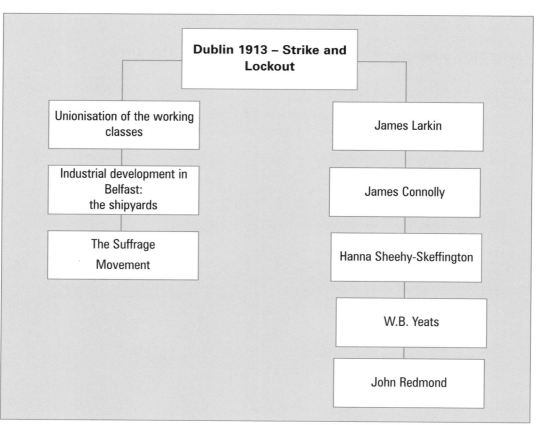

Dublin 1913 – Strike and Lockout

Unionisation of the working classes

Industrial development in Belfast:
the shipyards

The Suffrage Movement

James Larkin

James Connolly

Hanna Sheehy-Skeffington

W.B. Yeats

John Redmond

Topic: The Pursuit of Sovereignty and the Impact of Partition, 1912–49

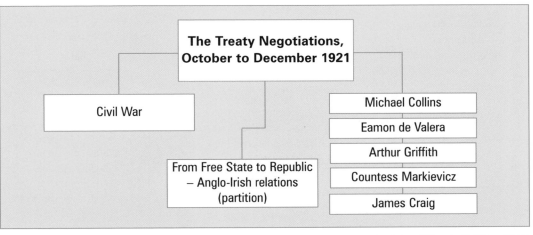

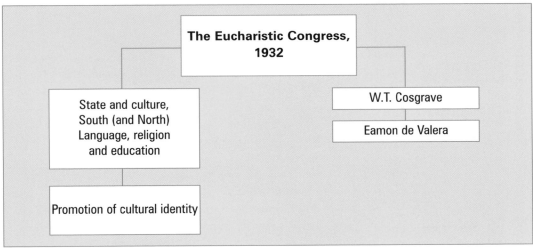

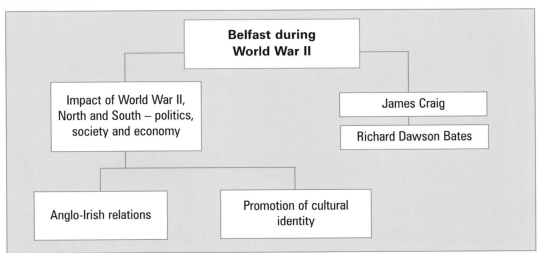

Topic: Government, Economy and Society in the Republic of Ireland, 1949–89

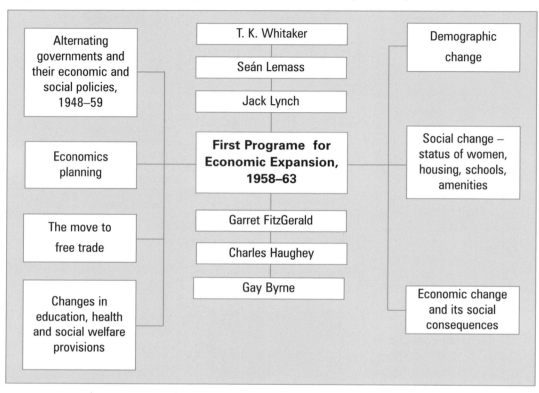

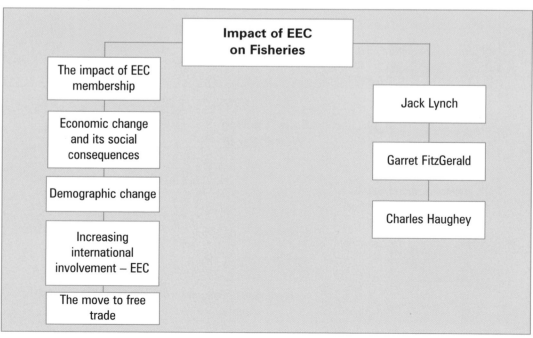

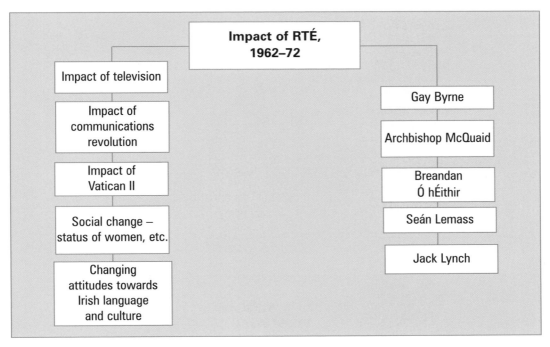

Impact of RTÉ, 1962–72

- Impact of television
- Impact of communications revolution
- Impact of Vatican II
- Social change – status of women, etc.
- Changing attitudes towards Irish language and culture

- Gay Byrne
- Archbishop McQuaid
- Breandan Ó hÉithir
- Seán Lemass
- Jack Lynch

Topic: Nation States and International Tensions, 1870–1920

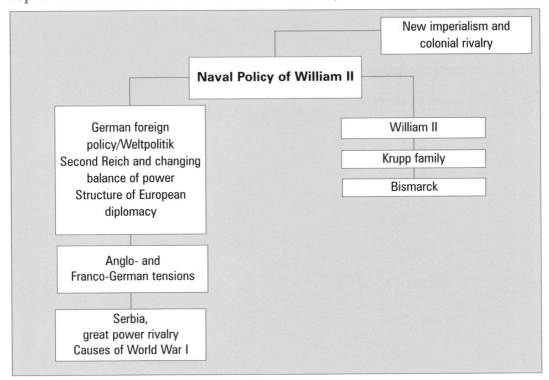

New imperialism and colonial rivalry

Naval Policy of William II

German foreign policy/Weltpolitik
Second Reich and changing balance of power
Structure of European diplomacy

- William II
- Krupp family
- Bismarck

Anglo- and Franco-German tensions

Serbia, great power rivalry
Causes of World War I

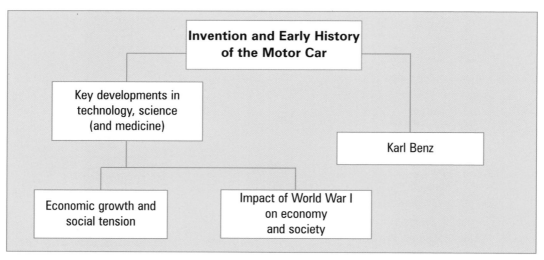

Invention and Early History of the Motor Car

Key developments in technology, science (and medicine)

Karl Benz

Economic growth and social tension

Impact of World War I on economy and society

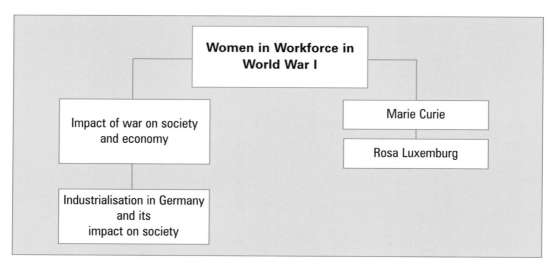

Women in Workforce in World War I

Impact of war on society and economy

Marie Curie

Rosa Luxemburg

Industrialisation in Germany and its impact on society

Topic: Dictatorship and Democracy in Europe, 1920–45

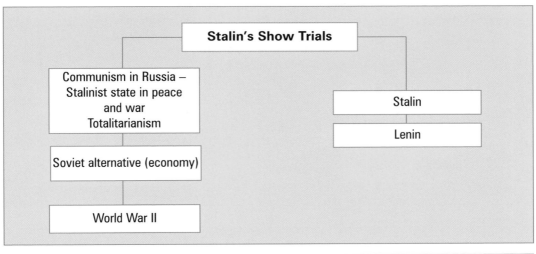

Stalin's Show Trials

Communism in Russia – Stalinist state in peace and war Totalitarianism

Soviet alternative (economy)

World War II

Stalin

Lenin

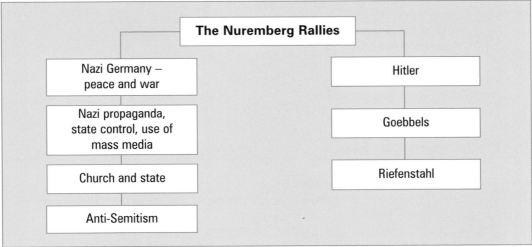

The Nuremberg Rallies

Nazi Germany – peace and war

Nazi propaganda, state control, use of mass media

Church and state

Anti-Semitism

Hitler

Goebbels

Riefenstahl

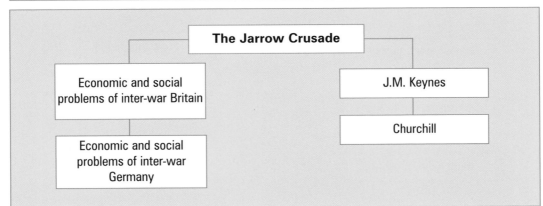

The Jarrow Crusade

Economic and social problems of inter-war Britain

Economic and social problems of inter-war Germany

J.M. Keynes

Churchill

Topic: Division and Realignment in Europe, 1945–92

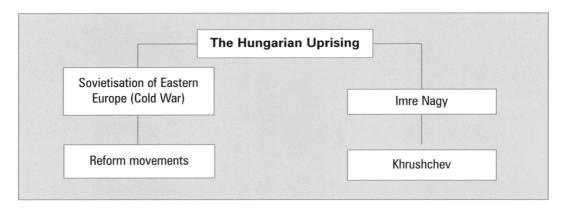

The Hungarian Uprising

Sovietisation of Eastern Europe (Cold War)

Imre Nagy

Reform movements

Khrushchev

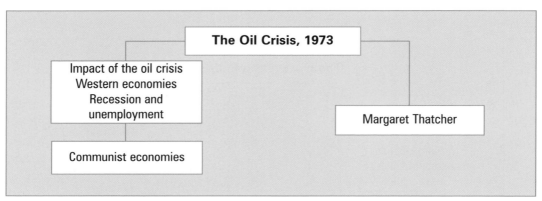

The Oil Crisis, 1973

Impact of the oil crisis
Western economies
Recession and
unemployment

Margaret Thatcher

Communist economies

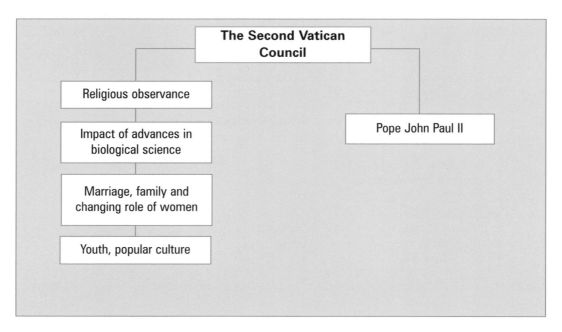

The Second Vatican Council

Religious observance

Impact of advances in biological science

Pope John Paul II

Marriage, family and changing role of women

Youth, popular culture

Sample Higher Level Essays and Sample Plans

MODERN IRISH HISTORY

Movements for Political and Social Reform, 1870–1914

Essay: What were the reasons for Irish unionist opposition to self-government for
Ireland, and what was the impact of that opposition on the course of Irish history
during the period 1886 to 1914?

Unionists were opposed to self-government for Ireland for economic, religious and
political reasons. Ulster, particularly Belfast, had prospered industrially under the Union.
Belfast's main industries, shipbuilding and linen, were dependent on the British market.
Unionists believed that a Dublin government would be more concerned with agriculture
than with industry, to the detriment of Ulster's prosperity. Protestants also feared that an
Irish parliament would be Catholic dominated and that their religious freedom would be
in danger – that Home Rule would be Rome Rule. In Ulster, there was an old tradition of
sectarian rivalry between Catholics and Protestants. Few on either side tolerated the other
side's point of view. The Secret Ballot Act of 1872 and the 1884 Reform Act reduced the
political power of the Protestants and they felt increasingly threatened. Protestants were in
a majority in the United Kingdom while the Union was maintained, but if Home Rule came
they would be in a minority in Ireland.

During 1885 to 1886, as Home Rule became a greater possibility, unionists and
Protestants became more and more agitated. In 1885, the Irish Loyal and Patriotic Union
was set up to fight Home Rule. In the general election of that year, two unionist MPs were
elected, both for the Trinity College Dublin constituency, while sixteen other unionist MPs
were elected in Ulster. The electorate was polarised into two groups – unionists and Home
Rulers. In Ulster, the Orange Order was revived; the Order was used to unite Protestants
of all classes in opposition to Home Rule. Ulster Unionists also started to make military
preparations to resist Home Rule. Many joined the Ulster Loyalist Anti-Repeal Union,
which was founded in January 1886. The Conservative Party in England decided to take
advantage of the situation in Ireland. The party saw Home Rule for Ireland as the first step
in the destruction of the Empire; it decided, in the words of Lord Randolph Churchill, that
'the Orange card would be the one to play', so an alliance was formed between the
unionists and the Conservative Party in England, which opposed the Liberal Alliance of
Parnell's party.

However, with the defeat of the Home Rule Bill in 1886 and the coming into power of the Conservatives, the danger of Home Rule diminished. When Home Rule became a possibility again after the 1892 election, Edward Saunderson, the MP for North Armagh, and others set up the Ulster Defence Union, which collected funds and made preparations to resist Home Rule. Even though the second Home Rule Bill passed the House of Commons, it was defeated in the Conservative-dominated House of Lords. Unionists were strongly opposed in 1904–05 to the Conservative proposal for devolution in Ireland. Although this only gave local government power to Ireland, unionists saw it as a stepping stone to Home Rule. They formed the Ulster Unionist Council in 1905 to co-ordinate the efforts of various Unionist organisations.

In December 1905, the Liberals came back to power and Home Rule was a possibility again. The new Liberal government had a large overall majority and did not need the support of the Home Rule Party. They did not consider Home Rule an urgent matter. However, Augustine Birrell, the Chief Secretary, brought in a Council bill somewhat similar to the earlier 'devolution' scheme. Redmond and the Home Rule Party rejected the bill but it kept unionist opposition to Home Rule on its toes. They needed to be alert because before the 1910 election, Asquith (Liberal prime minister), in return for promised Home Rule support, stated that Home Rule was the only possible solution to the Irish question. After the 1910 election, Redmond and the Irish Party held the balance of power at Westminster. By 1911 the Parliament Act deprived the House of Lords of its veto to stop Home Rule. From the unionist point of view, things looked very black.

Unionists began a sustained resistance to Home Rule. In September 1911 before a Home Rule Bill had been introduced in parliament, the unionist leader, Carson, addressed a huge meeting in Belfast. He proposed that unionists should ignore any Home Rule Act and that they should set up their own government, which would take office in the event of such an Act being passed. The Ulster Unionist Council then set about drafting a Constitution and preparing for self-government. Orangemen also began to drill and to arm. In 1912, unionists organised the Solemn League and Covenant. This was a pledge, signed by hundreds of thousands of unionists, to fight Home Rule 'by all means which may be found necessary'. In 1913, the Ulster Unionist Council founded the Ulster Volunteer Force (UVF); Sir George Richardson, a retired general, was appointed commander, but the UVF was not well armed. This was remedied by the Larne Gunrunning in April 1914, when thousands of rifles and millions of rounds of ammunition were landed at Larne, Bangor and Donaghadee. Unionists achieved another victory with the 'Curragh Mutiny' (1914), when fifty-eight officers indicated that they would resign rather than proceed against the unionists. The development of the Irish Volunteers in the South made the prospect of civil war more likely.

Unionist resistance forced compromise on the Home Rule issue between 1912 and 1914. Compromise proposals revolved around the permanent, or at least temporary, exclusion of all or part of the province of Ulster from the scope of the Home Rule Bill. Redmond and the Home Rule Party would not accept a partition. Neither did Carson favour partition, but Craig and many Ulster unionists were not particularly concerned about unionists in Southern Ireland and were prepared to accept partition. A conference of unionists, Home Rulers and British government representatives at Buckingham Palace in July 1914 failed to achieve agreement between the sides. The Home Rule Bill became law in September 1914 after the beginning of the First World War. But unionists had only accepted it on the understanding that it would not operate until after the war was over and the Ulster Question would then be reconsidered.

By the time the First World War was over in 1918, all had changed. Unionists and Home Rulers had fought together against Germany in the war, but this failed to unite them. Instead, the 1916 Rising and its aftermath changed the political situation in Ireland. During the War of Independence, the British government passed the Government of Ireland Act 1920, which set up a parliament in Belfast. This allowed unionists to control the six counties of Northern Ireland for most of the rest of the twentieth century. Unionist opposition to Home Rule failed to block independence for Southern Ireland, but it achieved a partial victory with the establishment of Northern Ireland.

Essay plan: Factors influencing the GAA/reasons for success

1. Organised sport: First organised games in 1800s spread to Ireland from England; played by gentlemen, Protestants, unionists and upper classes; only played on Saturdays, when poorer Catholics worked.

2. Progress of GAA: Founded 1884 – 600 clubs by 1887; spread like 'a prairie fire'; more popular in the countryside than cities (Dublin, Cork).

Reasons for success:

3. GAA's aims: organise Irish sports according to Irish rules – to draw up rules for the playing of these sports – to allow membership to all classes – an outlet for expressing Catholic and nationalist identities; growing sense of nationalism, opposed Anglicisation.

4. Organisation: Mirrored the growing organisation of Irish nationalism and structure of Irish politics; part of cultural revival (cultural nationalism) – benefited from links with Gaelic League – nationalist and popular patrons – Croke, Parnell, Davitt – encouraged publicity; Cusack full of energy, enthusiasm (already showed with success of Cusack's Academy) – clubs based on parishes, supported by Catholic clergy, helped by inter-parish rivalry and later inter-county rivalry; helped by spread of education for organising clubs.

5. Rules were published in national newspapers and in booklet form – numbers playing, goalposts, fouls – facilitated national competition – All-Ireland competitions.

6. Rural life: GAA filled a void – past–time, social function, matches on Sundays – only day without work, membership from farmers, farm labourers, barmen and shop assistants; later from teachers, clerks and civil servants.

7. Splits caused by influence of IRB – later resolved when GAA agreed to be non-political and non-sectarian.

Weaknesses – limits to success:

8. Cusack was a poor secretary, letters not replied to, receipts of club fees not provided, medals not awarded – forced to resign.

9. IRB presence and takeover – conflict with priests in parishes; conflict at GAA annual conventions, e.g. Thurles 1887 – Parnellite split – decline after 1891 – only six counties represented at annual convention in 1892.

10. Alienated Protestants/unionists: Games on Sundays, nationalist emphasis, ban on RIC and British army – increased division between Catholics and Protestants.

11. Financial problems: In debt of £400 by 1888; worsened by Davin's 'American invasion' – debt £1,000 by 1889.

12. Success after 1900: Improved rules and organisation provided training in democracy; inter-county teams played in the All-Ireland championships; encouraged growth of the separatist movement; GAA was another aspect of the wider cultural nationalism movement; use of the Irish language; in 1905 the ban on 'foreign games' was revived.

Essay plan: GAA and politics – IRB/republicanism/revival of nationalism

1. Background: Cusack – former IRB, Davin a committed nationalist; Cusack article in *United Ireland* wanted removal of 'foreign', British influence on games; patrons nationalists – Croke, Parnell, Davitt; GAA part of de-Anglicisation, cultural nationalism (revolt against Anglicisation, the importance of Irish identity and Irish culture); aims: stop the decline of native sports, open sports to all social classes, achieve Irish control of sport.

2. IRB: GAA seen as recruiting ground – at least two IRA members, Hoctor and Fitzgerald, were present at first meeting of GAA; Cusack was disliked by his assistant secretary, John Power, who was an IRB man; Cusack was forced to resign – 'inefficiency' – and replaced by another IRB man – new central council voted in – all IRB except the president, Davin – 1887 Convention, new IRB members set up dummy branches to give more power to IRB – IRB man Bennett appointed president – clashes between IRB and priests in parishes and

Dr Croke, Archbishop of Cashel – Croke resigned as patron to set up rival organisation with Davin – all members of central committee now members of county committees gave greater control to IRB.

3. Rules: Political motivation in rules – foreign games banned; banned RIC and British army members from joining GAA – clearly political; Protestants could not play on Sundays – mostly unionists so GAA nationalist – annual convention 1888: IRB realised the need for compromise; new convention agreed – IRB became a minority in Central Council – Davin back as president; Davin's 'American invasion' – Davin forced to resign as president – GAA also in financial difficulties – owed £400 in 1888, up to £1,000 in 1889 after failure of 'American Invasion'; GAA in decline – IRB still held control of county committees.

4. Parnell split: IRB took Parnell's side on leadership issue – Parnell appealed to extreme nationalists; GAA took Parnell's side, providing a guard of honour at his funeral; nearly destroyed the GAA – anti-Parnellites (majority) left GAA – number of clubs fell from 1,000 in 1888 to 220 in 1891 – six counties at annual convention in 1891.

5. After 1891: IRB remained in control but removed ban on RIC members (revived again in 1905) – GAA passed resolution that it was a non-political and non-sectarian organisation – emphasis on sport – growth in membership – more clubs, more counties at annual convention, priests involved, linked with Gaelic League – encouraged the Irish language, used Irish-made medals, etc; bought Jones's Road, which became Croke Park.

6. National identity: GAA helped create national identity – Gaelic and Catholic – contributed to spread of cultural nationalism – contributed to background of 1916 Rising and War of Independence; also growth of democracy.

Essay plan: GAA and wider cultural revival/cultural nationalism

1. Background: Decline of traditional games, spread of 'English' games.

2. Aims of GAA: Stop the decline of native sports, open sports to all social classes, achieve Irish control of sport.

3. Catholic and nationalist: Cusack and Davin, patrons, ban, Sundays, role of IRB, priests and parishes, success of matches.

4. Gaelic League: Decline of Irish language, revival of interest in Irish – foundation of Gaelic League – Hyde and 'Necessity for DeAnglicising Ireland' – language = the notes of nationalism.

5. Aims: Revive Irish as the national language; promote the study and publication of Irish literature; develop a new literature in Irish; de-Anglicise Ireland (by getting rid of other aspects of English culture).

6. Progress and success: Timirí, branches, in 1904 it had 600 league clubs with 50,000 members, newspaper, *An Claidheamh Soluis,* An t-Oireachtas, teacher training college, school for latter-day revolutionaries.

7. Anglo-Irish literary revival: Define – revival of Irish literature using the English language and based on Irish folktales, legends and history, Yeats, Lady Gregory, influence on nationalism, conflict with some nationalists.

Essay plans: 1913 Lockout

Larkin, Connolly and unionisation of the working classes

1. Living and working conditions in Belfast and Dublin: Dublin a trading city rather than an industrial one – 75 per cent of workers were unskilled – 'troublemakers' blacklisted – casual labour – workers only earned between 15 shillings and £1 – not enough to support a family – no trade unions to protect the workers – workers lived in decaying tenements – 20,000 families in one-roomed dwellings – sanitation was poor – one toilet in a yard – malnutrition – typhoid; **Belfast** – better-off than Dublin – casual and skilled labour – factories – skilled, well paid – craft unions – good-quality public housing.

2. Larkin in Belfast: Liverpool-born – Belfast organiser of National Union of Dock Labourers – very successful – strikes for recognition of union and higher wages, also in Cork and Derry; went to Dublin – sacked by superiors – founded Irish Transport and General Workers Union (ITGWU) in Dublin.

3. Larkin in Dublin: ITGWU had successful strikes for carters, dockers, railwaymen – increased membership to 10,000; campaign against heavy drinking – appointed Connolly official of ITGWU – employers hostile to ITGWU and Larkinism – W.M. Murphy founded Dublin Employers Federation.

4. Larkin's views on socialism and sympathetic strike: Wanted socialism – believed in syndicalism (workers unite in one great union) and sympathetic strike (workers supported other workers on strike by having nothing to do with employers of those on strike) – employers fear these views.

5. Tramway Co.: Murphy refused to allow employees in *Irish Independent* and Dublin Tramway Co. to join ITGWU – some tramway workers fired because of membership of ITGWU.

6. Strike and lockout: Larkin – strike – first day of Dublin Horse Show Week – 700 on strike – clashes with workers who continued working – clashes with police – one worker killed – sympathetic strike – other workers refuse to handle *Irish Independent*; speech by Larkin in Sackville St – disguised – Imperial Hotel – Larkin arrested – police baton-charge workers – other clashes later in city; employers draw up pledge – workers refuse to sign – dismissed.

7. Connolly: Worked for the Dublin Socialist Society – founded the Irish Socialist Republican Party (IRSP) – published a newspaper, *The Workers Republic*, in 1898 – linked the Social Question and the National Question – favoured public (government) ownership of the means of production – nationalisation (government ownership) of railways and canals – founded Irish Labour Party with Larkin 1912 – union official in ITGWU – set up Citizens Army during lockout – 250 members – to protect workers – in charge of strike when Larkin was in jail – took more moderate approach – said lockout was a 'drawn battle' – General Secretary of ITGWU after Larkin left for America in 1914 – anti-WWI – 1916 Rising.

8. British unions: Delegates from Dublin ask British TUC for help – sent food – food ship *The Hare* sent with 60,000 family boxes – food kitchens in Liberty Hall – Larkin to England – speeches – some sympathetic strikes – British union leaders against – conflict with Larkin – **Askwith Inquiry** failed to solve dispute – Larkin on second tour of England – Fiery Cross Campaign – failed to get general British stoppage – workers weakening – return to work slowly in January 1914.

9. Impact of lockout on unions: Employers believed they had smashed Larkinism, but ITGWU survived – became largest union in Dublin (and country) – bitterness between workers and employers, and police – founding of Irish Citizens Army during lockout – took part in 1916 Rising – awareness of living and working conditions – Larkin left for America – did not return until 1923.

Essay plan: Industrial development and unionisation of the working classes

1. Industrial development in Ireland: Concentrated in the north-east, especially Belfast; in the south based mostly on processing agricultural produce, e.g. Guinness, Jamesons – a lack of infrastructure, raw materials and skilled workers – industry failed to modernise and faced competition from mass-produced British goods; a shrinking market with a decreasing Irish population.

2. Industry in Dublin: Mainly a centre of commerce and trade – failed to develop in industry like much of the rest of Ireland; decline of local industry – fall in demand for skilled workers; **Industry in Belfast:** Belfast Harbour dredged and Queen's Island formed; deep harbour to accommodate larger ships (liners from shipyards, etc.); good supply of labour migrating from rest of Ulster; industrialists and entrepreneurs willing to invest in and adapt new technology (Harland & Wolff shipbuilding methods); British demand for ships (Wolff link to Liverpool shipping companies who bought Harland & Wolff ships).

3. Working classes in Dublin: Difficult to organise – involved in unskilled, casual labour; men hired on a daily basis, low pay, easily replaced; women worked mostly as domestic servants, were isolated and difficult to unionise; the working classes lived in poor conditions, one family per room in three- or four-storey tenements – workers could not afford union membership, also poorly educated.

4. Working classes in Belfast: A mix of casual and skilled labour – worked in factories and places of mass employment (easier to organise); workmen were highly skilled, well paid and had pride in craft (welders, riveters, carpenters, fitters) – not easily replaced and had craft unions to protect them; women worked in textile factories and were poorly paid, but easier to organise than women workers in Dublin – workers lived in good-quality housing.

Role of Larkin and Connolly:

5. Larkin in Belfast: Liverpool-born – Belfast organiser of National Union of Dock Labourers – very successful – strikes for recognition of union and higher wages, also in Cork and Derry; went to Dublin – sacked by superiors – founded Irish Transport and General Workers Union (ITGWU) in Dublin.

6. Larkin in Dublin: ITGWU had successful strikes for carters, dockers, railwaymen – increased membership to 10,000; campaign against heavy drinking – appointed Connolly official of ITGWU – employers hostile to ITGWU and Larkinism – W.M. Murphy founded Dublin Employers Federation.

7. Larkin's views on socialism and sympathetic strike: Wanted socialism – believed in syndicalism (workers unite in one great union) and sympathetic strike (workers supported other workers on strike by having nothing to do with employers of those on strike) – employers fear these views.

8. Larkin's role in Dublin Strike and Lockout (see below).

9. Connolly: Worked for the Dublin Socialist Society – founded the Irish Socialist Republican Party (IRSP) – published a newspaper, *The Workers Republic*, in 1898 – linked the Social Question and the National Question – favoured public (government) ownership of the means of production – nationalisation (government ownership) of railways and canals – founded Irish Labour Party with Larkin 1912 – union official in ITGWU – set up Citizens Army during lockout – 250 members to protect workers – in charge of strike when Larkin was in jail – took more moderate approach – said lockout was a 'drawn battle' – General Secretary of ITGWU after Larkin left for America in 1914 – anti-WWI – 1916 Rising.

Essay plan: Larkin and Murphy – role in 1913 Strike and Lockout

1. **Larkin:** Speaker, union organiser – use of sympathetic strike – socialism – ITGWU.
2. **Murphy:** Owner of *Irish Independent*, Imperial Hotel, Dublin Tramway Co. – founded Dublin Employers Federation to resist ITGWU and 'Larkinism' – fear of.
3. **Tramway Co:** Larkin recruits workers – Murphy spoke to workers – some sacked (100) – sympathetic strike against Easons for handling *Irish Independent*.
4. **Horse Show Week:** Larkin on strike, lockout by Murphy – press interviews by each criticised the other.
5. **Bloody Sunday:** Sackville St meeting banned by government – Larkin in disguise – Imperial Hotel – significance of – arrested – police baton-charge workers.
6. **Pledge:** Murphy and employers insist on pledge by workers not to join ITGWU; more workers locked out – by September, 20,000 workers locked out or on strike.
7. **British help:** Food sent – £100,000 in aid – Larkin on speaking tours of England – wanted sympathetic strikes – Murphy got support from Home Rulers and Catholic nationalists – fear of Larkinism, e.g. the Kiddies Scheme to take children to England.
8. **No compromise:** Murphy did not want to give in or compromise – refused to accept suggestions of Askwith Inquiry – Larkin went to England again to get help – Fiery Cross Campaign – wanted a widespread sympathetic strike – union leaders there refused.
9. **Return to work:** Workers hungry, ITGWU can't support them; Larkin and ITGWU agree to end strike – urge workers to go back – not to sign pledge if possible – Murphy claimed victory and end of Larkinism – but right of workers to organise unions won – Larkin left for America – highlighted living and working conditions.

The Pursuit of Sovereignty and the Impact of Partition, 1912–49

Essay plan: What progress did the Irish Free State make in the pursuit of sovereignty between the Treaty of 1921 and the declaration of the Republic in 1949?

Intro: Treaty terms, oath, Governor-General, ports, Privy Council, Northern Ireland.
1. Cumann na nGaedheal, restless dominion, independent foreign policy, examples.
2. Boundary Commission, failure, why? Partition.
3. Imperial conferences, Balfour Declaration, Statute of Westminster.
4. De Valera and dismantling the treaty, examples.
5. New Constitution, Anglo-Irish Agreement, treaty ports.

6. WWII, neutrality, dangers to, success.

Conclusion: Republic of Ireland Act 1949.

The following essay has been developed from the above essay plan.

Essay: What progress did the Irish Free State make in the pursuit of sovereignty between the Treaty of 1921 and the declaration of the Republic in 1949?

After the Anglo-Irish Treaty of 1921, Ireland had partial independence. The South was a dominion of the British Commonwealth; three Treaty ports (Lough Swilly, Berehaven and Queenstown) were controlled by Britain, along with six counties in the North. The British king was head of state, with TDs having to swear an oath of allegiance to him. He was represented by the Governor-General in Ireland. So despite Southern Ireland now being called the 'Free State', it was still under the influence of Britain. However, over the next three decades, various Irish governments expanded Ireland's independence in their pursuit of sovereignty.

Ireland was known as the 'Restless Dominion'. Always eager to assert its independence, the Cumann na nGaedheal government saw the Anglo-Irish Treaty as a stepping stone to full independence. Ireland was different to other dominions in many respects. The Irish government saw dominion status as second best. The Governor-General (Tim Healy) was an Irishman and a commoner and the oath of allegiance taken by the TDs was less royal than other oaths. Indeed, Ireland's geographical closeness to Britain spurred her on even more in her search for full independence. An indicator of this desire for independence was Ireland's membership of the League of Nations in 1923. In 1924, Ireland registered the Anglo-Irish Treaty with the League, thus making it an agreement between two sovereign governments. Furthermore, Ireland sent her own representatives to the USA, France and Germany. Even though the steps taken were minor ones, they were important in showing the world that Ireland was serious in its pursuit of sovereignty.

However, in spite of the Free State's enthusiasm, it did suffer some setback in its pursuit of sovereignty, namely the Boundary Commission. In 1924, a Boundary Commission was set up to determine exactly where the border between the Free State and Northern Ireland should lay. Its chairman was J.R. Feetham from South Africa, the Northern representative was J.R. Fisher, a unionist, and the Southern representative was Eoin McNeill, Minister for Education. However, the Commission was ignored by Craig, the Northern prime minister. Feetham, significantly, decided that the border should be determined by geographical and economic considerations rather than the wishes of the people. The Free State was in danger of losing parts of Donegal and gaining only a small part of Armagh and Fermanagh. To stop the Boundary Commission report being made public, Cosgrave, O'Higgins and McGilligan hurried to London. The border remained as it was and partition was made permanent. The South failed to extend its sovereignty over any part of Northern Ireland.

The Cumann na nGaedheal government, however, made good use of the Imperial Conferences to extend the power and influence of the dominions. This led to the Balfour Declaration in 1926, which stated that all dominions were 'autonomous, equal in status, in no way subordinate to one another'. This was followed by the Statute of Westminster in 1931, which meant that the dominions could make their own laws and repeal ones made previously by Britain. Now the Free State was in a position to alter the Treaty, leaving it to pursue total independence.

De Valera made good use of the Statute of Westminster when he came to power. He set about dismantling the Treaty in a step-by-step manner. Firstly, he abolished the oath of allegiance, which was followed by the demotion of the Governor–General, James MacNeill. He was replaced by Dómhnaill Ó Buachalla, a former Fianna Fáil candidate, who made a mockery of the post. The post was finally abolished in 1936. The abdication of King Edward VIII helped de Valera in the pursuit of sovereignty, as he was able to remove all remaining functions of the king from the constitution. He passed the External Relations Act, which allowed the king to appoint diplomatic representatives. In this way, de Valera had achieved 'external association' with Britain. De Valera consolidated the changes in a new Constitution, passed in 1937. This Constitution made Ireland a republic in all but name.

There were threats to Ireland's sovereignty. The Economic War highlighted Ireland's financial dependence on Britain. It was brought to an end by the Anglo-Irish Agreement. In this agreement, the Treaty ports were handed back to Ireland, which was highly significant in maintaining Ireland's neutrality during WWII. Indeed, WWII posed its own problems in regard to Irish sovereignty. Several of the Great Powers threatened Ireland, including Britain. Britain demanded the Treaty ports be returned, but de Valera refused. Churchill promised if Ireland entered the war, partition would be ended after the war. Again de Valera refused, as he knew he could not convince the unionists. At the end of the war, Churchill criticised de Valera, but de Valera's reply reflected the confidence of a country which had expanded and maintained its sovereignty.

The Inter-Party Government took the final step in pursuit of sovereignty by declaring Ireland a republic in 1949 (the Republic of Ireland Act) and leaving the British Commonwealth. However, this action, along with the Ireland Act, passed by Britain, reinforced partition, thereby limiting sovereignty to the twenty-six counties. Nevertheless, over the previous twenty-seven years, Ireland had made immense progress in her pursuit of sovereignty. The country had made the transition from dominion to republic, never compromising, even in the face of danger or when she suffered setback.

Government, Economy and Society in the Republic of Ireland, 1949–89

Essay: What were the successes and failures of the First Inter-Party Government, 1948–51?

In 1948, de Valera, Taoiseach and leader of Fianna Fáil, called a snap general election. Even though Fianna Fáil won the largest number of seats, the First Inter-Party Government was formed after the election. Fianna Fáil lost support because emergency conditions continued after the war. There was also high unemployment and emigration and many people felt a change was needed after sixteen years. This was particularly the case with the opposition parties, who wanted to get de Valera out. Consequently, Fine Gael, Labour, Clann na Poblachta, Clann na Talmhan, National Labour and Independents came together to form the First Inter-Party Government. Indeed, their first success was in forming the government as Mulcahy, leader of Fine Gael, allowed John A. Costello to become Taoiseach because he himself was not favoured by the other parties.

The First Inter-Party Government faced a number of economic problems, such as an exodus from the land, lack of manufacturing industry, unemployment and emigration. The problems of agriculture were given to James Dillon as Minister of Agriculture. He initiated the Land Rehabilitation Project, which aimed to reclaim 1.5 million hectares of land. This cost £40 million and the money was obtained from ERP (European Recovery Programme – Marshall Aid/Plan). Dillon also got a Trade Agreement with Britain (1948), which provided better prices for sheep and cattle. He also began a scheme of reafforestation, which increased planting from 2,000 hectares a year to 10,000 hectares a year. He promoted rural electrification, which continued during 1950s – this gave farmers the opportunity to use more machinery. Overall, the agriculture policy of the First Inter-Party Government was successful, though rural depopulation continued.

The government promoted manufacturing industry through a policy of encouraging state investment. An economic plan was drawn up (1949) to benefit from Marshall Aid. ERP money was used to set up Coras Tráchtála to promote exports in the USA and Canada, and the Industrial Development Authority (IDA) was set up to promote industry in Ireland. Through its Public Capital Programme, the government built houses, hospitals and schools. This increased employment to cater for the outflow of people from agriculture. The GNP (gross national product) increased by 3 per cent each year from 1947 to 1951. The manufacturing industry was still protected so it produced for the home market and not for export. Even though 70,000 people left agriculture, they mostly got employment, as 50,000 jobs were created in Irish industry. Consequently, unemployment fell from 9.3 per cent (1947) to 7.3 per cent (1951), but emigration was higher. The government's policy had helped improve the economy.

The Inter-Party Government had mixed fortunes in foreign policy. The government repealed the External Relations Act 1936 and passed the Republic of Ireland Act 1949, which declared Ireland a republic. Ireland formally became a republic in Easter 1949. Even though Costello hoped that this would take the gun out of Irish politics, this did not happen. However, relations with Britain remained good. The British government passed the British Nationality Act, which said that Irish citizens would have the same rights and privileges as British citizens. But pressure from Northern unionists led to the passage of the Ireland Act 1949, which said Northern Ireland would remain part of the UK so long as the parliament of Northern Ireland wished to. This reinforced partition and upset the Inter-Party Government.

The government now began an anti-partition policy of pressurising Britain to leave the North. The government was supported by opposition parties, including Fianna Fáil. Irish delegates at foreign conferences spoke about 'the evils of partition'. But European delegates were irritated by these comments; they were more concerned about the effects of World War II. The anti-partition policy was a failure. However, the government continued to maintain the traditional policy of neutrality. McBride, Minister of External Affairs, refused to join NATO (North Atlantic Treaty Organisation). But Ireland did support the US in the Cold War against the 'atheistic communism' of the USSR. Ireland also joined the Organisation for European Economic Co-operation (OEEC) and the Council of Europe. But the government did not join the ECSC (European Coal and Steel Community) because of Ireland's trade relationship with Britain, which also did not join. Overall, the Inter-Party Government, while maintaining the traditional policy towards Britain, also widened Irish foreign policy.

The government's health policy had both successes and failures. The new Minister of Health, Dr Noel Browne, was faced with a major problem of TB, as there were 3,000 to 4,000 deaths a year from it. This was caused by poverty, malnutrition and bad housing and worsened by the war conditions. The government built 12,000 houses annually to clear the backlog of 110,000 houses. This, along with improvements in water and sewage for existing houses, contributed to improving public health. But it was the policies of Browne which were mainly responsible for eradicating TB. He organised a systematic campaign – 2,000 extra hospital beds were provided, there were mobile X-ray units to identify TB sufferers, TB patients were given free medical treatment and the BCG injection was used. Browne got £20 million from the Irish Hospitals Sweepstakes Funds and borrowed £10 million. As a result of this campaign, TB cases dropped by nearly half by 1951 and improvement continued during the 1950s.

However, Browne's more ambitious proposal for a Mother and Child Scheme was a failure. He proposed free medical treatment for children under sixteen and for mothers, without a means test. This proposal provoked strong opposition from the IMA (Irish Medical Association), who were against state control of medicine. The IMA feared that doctors would lose income and said the scheme would interfere with the doctor–patient relationship. Equally strong opposition came from the Catholic Church, who looked on it as communism and saw it as a threat to faith and morals. The Cabinet was also opposed to the scheme because of the fear of the Catholic Church and because Browne did not consult colleagues on occasions. Even Browne's own leader, McBride, thought Browne was too radical. When Browne failed to win over the Catholic bishops, the Cabinet refused to back him. McBride demanded his resignation when he refused to compromise and Browne resigned in April 1951. The affair weakened the Inter-Party Government – Browne and two other deputies withdrew their support from the government – but it did not lead to its collapse.

Instead, economic problems were mostly to blame – inflation, the balance of payments (more imports than exports) problems and the failure to increase the price of milk to farmers eventually led to the fall of the First Inter-Party Government. The government failed to get elected in the general election of 1951, but it had many successes to its credit. Its economic, social and health policies were relatively successful, and it was the first government to make an effort at economic planning, for example. But it also had other successes. The existence of coalition healed some of the bitterness of the Civil War because it brought together people of different political backgrounds. Through it, Fine Gael regained confidence and the Labour Party was reunited. Undoubtedly, the success of the First Inter-Party Government contributed to the return to power of the Second Inter-Party Government three years later in 1954.

Essay: What was the contribution of Seán Lemass to the modernisation of the Irish state?

Seán Lemass was a pragmatist who, like de Valera, believed that Sinn Féin should come in from the political wilderness. He followed de Valera in leaving Sinn Féin and was a founder member of Fianna Fáil in May 1926. Seán Lemass, together with Gerald Boland, played a key role in building up the organisation of the new party at local constituency level. When Fianna Fáil entered the Dáil in 1927, Lemass took a leading part in opposing the Cumann na nGaedheal government. His work in building up Fianna Fáil strengthened democracy and moved the country away from physical force towards a modern democratic state.

Following the 1932 general election, Fianna Fáil entered government and Lemass was appointed Minister for Industry and Commerce. At this time, he advocated the old Sinn Féin policy of economic self-sufficiency and protectionism. During the 1930s, he put in place a programme of tariff protection for Irish industry and state intervention to develop the country's resources. He established a number of semi-state bodies, including Bord na Móna and Aer Lingus. Despite the depression of the 1930s, Lemass's achievement in generating industrial growth was remarkable. Employment in industry rose from 110,000 in 1932 to 166,000 in 1938. This was another stage in the development of a more modern industrial structure in the country.

During World War II, Lemass was appointed Minister for Supplies. He had responsibility for rationing and controlling the distribution of limited resources such as petrol and foodstuffs. His energy, pragmatism and organisational ability made him well suited for this task. His work contributed to maintaining Irish neutrality and independence.*

During the 1950s, Lemass was again appointed Minister for Industry and Commerce in the two de Valera governments of 1951–54 and 1957–59. He became increasingly convinced of the need for Irish industry to become competitive in a market economy based on free trade. He believed that the protectionist policies of the past were in need of radical review. Lemass strongly supported the economic policy proposed by T.K. Whitaker, Secretary of the Department of Finance. The government adopted Whitaker's proposals in November 1958 in the First Programme for Economic Expansion. Lemass provided the political will to implement this programme when he succeeded de Valera as Taoiseach and leader of Fianna Fáil in 1959.

The First Programme for Economic Expansion was a watershed in the development of the Irish economy. It set targets for growth and attracted foreign industries to Ireland by means of generous grants and tax concessions. The results were spectacular: output increased by almost one-quarter, unemployment fell by one-third and emigration declined sharply. Much of Ireland's economic transformation and modernisation was due to Lemass's leadership and vision.

Lemass believed that Irish industry should become more competitive within Europe and he applied for Irish membership of the EEC in 1961 as part of a joint application with Britain. However, as a result of France's opposition to Britain's application for membership, Ireland did not become a member of the EEC until 1973. Nevertheless, Lemass sought to maximise Ireland's economic advantage abroad by joining the European Free Trade Association and concluding an Anglo-Irish Trade Agreement in 1965. This helped get the country ready for further modernisation.

Lemass also brought new thinking to the problem of Northern Ireland. In 1965, he had two historic meetings with the prime minister of Northern Ireland, Captain Terence O'Neill. These meetings indicated a willingness to develop a more open relationship between the governments of North and South. He also contributed to expanding Ireland's role in international affairs by participation in the United Nations, in particular in active peacekeeping missions.

As Taoiseach from 1959 to 1966, Lemass presided over a period of unprecedented economic and social change in Ireland. He brought a new, pragmatic managerial style to the Irish economy. In encouraging competitiveness and openness to change, he moved the Irish economy away from the stagnation of the past. Although remaining strongly nationalist, he also believed that Ireland's future would be best served by developing closer links with the outside world. Throughout his political career, he was involved in and often led the major changes which modernised the Irish state.

Note: There are no dates in this essay title, so the first three paragraphs are relevant to the title. If dates, e.g. 'from 1949 onwards', were included in the title, then the first three paragraphs here should be condensed into one (the introduction).

MODERN EUROPE AND THE WIDER WORLD

Nation States and International Tensions, 1871–1920

Essay plan: How important was the contribution of Karl Benz to the invention and early history of the motor car?

Intro: Steam and electric cars, slow, resistance to, problems, rapid change between 1870s and 1890s, Benz a vital role.

1. Benz's work: Mechanical engineer, internal combustion engine, three-wheeled car, motorwagen, open two-seater body, tiller, speed, horse carriage, patent for first petrol-driven car, horseless carriage, sold first car to Paris.

2. Benz's work: Company, world's first car manufacturer, 1888 had fifty workers, three-wheeled car, moved to four-wheeled car, Benz Velo, 1,220 cars, 400 workers, 1899 saw 572 cars produced, world's largest car manufacturer, 1903 retired, kept interest until death in 1929.

3. Wife's contribution: Bertha more business orientated, used dowry, drove first car through Mannheim, drove longest car journey yet, 100 km, Mannheim to Stuttgart, advert for cars.

4. Other inventors: Otto – first internal combustion engine, four stroke petrol powered, Benz based his engine on this; Daimler – first four-wheeled car, improved engine, passed out Benz, companies joined as Daimler-Benz in 1926.

5. Other inventors: Diesel – new type of engine, improvements to steering wheel, pneumatic tyre, disc brakes, four-wheel braking; lighter engine, faster, engine in front, road races for testing.

6. Ford: Assembly line production, standardised parts, later copied by Europeans, mass production; impact of WWI – need for more reliable, stronger car.

Conclusion: One of many, but made key contributions, depended on work of others, e.g. Otto, Bertha, passed out by other improvements; impact of car on economy and society – brief mention.

Dictatorship and Democracy in Europe, 1920–45

Essay plan: Totalitarian state/dictatorship – Stalin holding onto power – the purges and show trials

Lenin: Created communist dictatorship during Russian Civil War – increased party membership (almost trebled), set up Cheka (secret service), used Red Terror to eliminate all opposition, banned all opposition parties, all state power concentrated in hands of Party members.

You can use information on Lenin if the question concerns the development of a totalitarian state/dictatorship in the Soviet Union, 1920–39.

Intro: Struggle for power, grey blur, General Secretary, versus Trotsky, later Zinoviev and Kamenev, permanent revolution versus socialism in one country, Politburo filled with Stalin supporters by 1929.

1. Totalitarian state: Appearance of democratic structure – freedom of speech/press, right to vote, etc.; but totalitarian dictatorship – controlled by Communist Party; use of NKVD secret service; Soviet army controlled by Party; cult of personality – worship of Stalin promoted; history rewritten; posters, photographs, statues, cities renamed, treated like a god; consolidated his power.

2. Beginning of purges – assassination of Kirov: Increased opposition to Stalin due to collectivisation and industrialisation; fear of Trotsky even though in exile; Kirov – popular Party leader in Leningrad; assassination blamed on a plot; Stalin's involvement? Assassin and others killed, hundreds soon after – witch hunt; consolidated Stalin's power.

3. Great Purge – First Show Trial (Trial of the 16) August 1936: Zinoviev and Kamenev arrested; accused of being Trotskyites, killing Kirov and plotting to kill Stalin; organised by Yagoda, head of NKVD; forced confessions; Vyshinsky, prosecutor; found guilty; executed next day in Lubyanka prison; Stalin consolidated power by eliminating old Bolsheviks, others suspected of loyalty to Trotsky.

4. Second Show Trial (Trial of the 17) January 1937: Pyatakov, Radek and fifteen others – former supporters of Trotsky; same charges as previous trial; confessions; most condemned to death, Radek to long prison sentence; secret purge of Red Army – executed top commanders, including Marshal Tukhachevsky and half officer corps shot or jailed; Stalin consolidated power by eliminating enemies, but weakened the army and almost led to downfall of Soviet Union at beginning of WWII.

5. Third Show Trial (Trial of 21) March 1938: Bukharin, Rykov (former members of Lenin's Politburo) and Yagoda (former head of secret service); organised by Yezhov ('Yezhovshchina'), new head of secret service; accused of plotting with Trotsky, planning to kill Stalin, wrecking the economy; confessions; executed; Stalin consolidated power with elimination of last remaining threats.

6. Stalin's role: Directed the interrogations and trials; attended some secretly; Stalin not linked to show trials; outsiders (e.g. US ambassador) viewed show trials as properly conducted – they showed evidence of conspiracy; widespread coverage in press; full extent of Stalin's involvement not publicly known until Khrushchev made speech at 20th Party Congress (1956).

7. Continuation of Purges: Local Party officials purged; millions of ordinary Russians; general fear; sent to Siberia – gulags (labour camps) or death; accused of plotting with Nazi Germany or 'Japanese hirelings'.

Conclusion: No challenge to rule of Stalin; new generation of leaders loyal to Stalin, e.g. Khrushchev; purges slowed down Five Year Plans and collectivisation; weakened the Red Army; but disciplined Soviet population; increased control of Stalin; also used propaganda (cult of personality).

Essay: What factors contributed to the rise of fascism in Europe in the inter-war years, 1920–39?

In the inter-war years, 1920–39, there was a growth of dictatorship throughout Europe. Some of these were fascist dictatorships. This was particularly the case in Italy and Germany, where fascism had its only long-lasting successes. Indeed, it was in Italy that fascism was born. As a political philosophy, fascism stood for anti-communism, extreme nationalism, racism, totalitarianism and expansionism in foreign policy. Even though its main successes were Italy and Germany, it spread to other countries, such as Britain and Spain. However, by the end of the Second World War, it had largely disappeared.

The First World War contributed significantly to the growth of fascism. In Italy, for example, nationalists were disappointed at the failure to acquire Fiume and Dalmatia at the Paris Peace Conference. In response to this, D'Annunzio took over Fiume for a short-lived fascist-style dictatorship. His action contributed to the rise to power of Mussolini's Fascist Party. The peace treaties also caused problems for Germany. The harsh terms of the Treaty of Versailles undermined support for the democratic Weimar Republic and increased the popularity of Hitler's Nazi Party. In particular, the problem of reparations (the payment of £6.6 billion compensation for war damage) helped Hitler become a national politician rather than a local Bavarian politician when he opposed the Young Plan referendum in 1929.

The economic effects of World War I also contributed to the growth of fascism. Huge numbers of demobilised soldiers returned home to unemployment. In Italy in 1919, there were 2 million unemployed. They also experienced rapid inflation, so hunger and poverty were their only thanks for their wartime suffering. These men formed the backbone of Mussolini's Fascio di Combattimento, who beat up socialists and communists and crushed strikers. In Germany, Hitler attempted his putsch in Munich as the country experienced hyperinflation caused by the French invasion of the Ruhr to seek reparations. But Hitler had to wait for the much worse economic conditions of the Great Depression before he eventually achieved power.

In 1929, the Wall Street crash led to the Great Depression. As American banks and industries collapsed, America called back loans which had been given to Germany. These loans formed the basis of German prosperity in the second half of the 1920s. Consequently, their withdrawal resulted in the closure of German factories and a rise in unemployment from 1.5 million in 1929 to over 6 million in 1932. The moderate German middle class and farmers were pushed towards the extreme politics of Nazism. Hitler's party increased its support from twelve seats in the Reichstag in 1928 to becoming the largest party in 1932.

Faced by huge political and economic problems, the existing democratic parties and governments could not stop the rise of fascism. Italy experienced rapid changes of government between 1919 and 1922, while the Weimar Republic in Germany averaged a new government every nine months. In Italy, King Victor Emmanuel III tired of the weak governments. After the March on Rome, he looked to the strong government of Mussolini to solve Italy's problems. In Germany, the Weimar governments were forced to rule by decree to bring in unpopular measures to cope with the Great Depression. The use of Article 48 signalled the failure of democracy and the approach of Hitler's dictatorship.

The fascist parties also contributed to their own growth by the appeal of their policies, their leadership style and their use of propaganda. This can be clearly seen in Mussolini's rise to power in Italy. His use of the Blackshirts, the straight arm salute, marches and parades gave an impression of strength. He was also an outstanding speaker. In Germany, Hitler used similar propaganda techniques. He believed that when you tell a lie, tell a big lie. Hitler's policies also had wide appeal to the nationalists, the middle class and the industrialists.

Both Mussolini and Hitler were appointed prime ministers democratically – Mussolini after he planned the March on Rome, Hitler with the help of right-wing plotting. But both leaders then used the power of the state to create fascist dictatorships. Through the Acerbo Law (the party with the majority of votes in the election got two-thirds of the seats), the Aventine Secession and rule by decree, Mussolini had set up a dictatorship by 1925. Hitler followed a similar path. He used the Reichstag Fire, the 1933 general election, the Enabling Act (rule by decree) and the death of President Hindenburg to create his dictatorship. Both also used state propaganda to ensure greater control.

Once fascism came to power, it continued to expand. Mussolini used wars in Libya and Abyssinia to take over more land. Hitler broke the Treaty of Versailles by remilitarising the Rhineland, taking over Austria (Anschluss) and the Sudetenland. Eventually Hitler's expansionism led to the Second World War, which resulted in the downfall of both dictatorships and the end of the fascists in power. Fascism contained within itself the seeds of its own destruction.

Essay: To what extent did Germany's social and economic problems lead to the rise of Hitler and the Nazis?

After the First World War, the Weimar Republic was established in Germany. It was a democratic government which faced many political, social and economic problems. However, by the mid-1920s, the German economy had improved and Germany was accepted back into the European family of nations through the Locarno Pact. But the Weimar Republic collapsed in 1933 when Hitler and the Nazis came to power. Hitler's rise to power continued after this, as he rapidly wiped out the last traces of Weimar democracy. He achieved power by exploiting the new social and economic problems which Germany experienced after 1929.

The rise of Hitler and the Nazis owed much to the Great Depression. In 1929, the value of shares in the New York Stock Exchange in Wall Street collapsed. Americans called in loans they had given to Germany and so German companies went bankrupt. Unemployment in Germany rose from 1.5 million in 1929 to 6 million in 1932. Middle- and working-class families were badly hit. Some joined the Nazi Party, while others supported the Party because they saw it as the solution to Germany's economic problems. Hitler's support came largely from the middle classes who feared the rise of communism.

Hitler and the Nazis were helped by the weaknesses of the Weimar government. The Weimar government was unpopular because it was associated with defeat in the First World War and the harsh Treaty of Versailles. The leaders of the Republic were called the 'November criminals'. The ruling classes (judges, generals) of the old German empire favoured authoritarian government and undermined the Weimar Republic. Judges, for example, were lenient on right-wing troublemakers, such as Hitler after the Munich putsch. The government added to its problems by failing to deal with the social and economic problems caused by the Great Depression. In fact, it made them worse by cutting back on government spending, which increased unemployment. The Weimar government also undermined democracy by using President Hindenburg's power to rule by decree.

Hitler and the Nazis used tactics and policies to exploit the effects of the Great Depression and the weaknesses of the Weimar government. After the failure of the Munich putsch, Hitler wanted to use democracy to destroy democracy. 'If outvoting them takes longer than outshooting them, then at least the result will be guaranteed by their own constitution,' he said. Hitler developed branches of the Nazi Party all over Germany and appointed district leaders such as Goebbels in Berlin. He also used the SA (Brownshirts – Storm Troopers) and SS (Blackshirts) to attack opponents, particularly socialists and communists.

Hitler's policies attracted support from many different groups in Germany. He got support from nationalists, industrialists, farmers and the lower middle class, and less so from the working class, who supported the communists. Hitler outlined his ideas in *Mein Kampf*, his autobiography. He got the support of nationalists by attacking the Treaty of Versailles and promising to unite all German-speaking people. He won the support of other groups by his strong anti-communism and his promise to solve Germany's economic problems.

Hitler and his Reich propaganda leader, Goebbels, used propaganda to get across their policies. Hitler was an outstanding speaker who knew how to control a crowd. Goebbels organised the propaganda for elections and used newspapers, airplanes, films and loudspeakers from trucks to gain greater support. The Nazis also used uniforms, salutes and mass rallies to appear strong. Not surprisingly, support for Hitler and the Nazi Party grew quickly. In 1928, they held twelve seats in the Reichstag; by 1930 they had over 100 seats and in July 1932 they became the largest party, with 230 seats. Hitler also showed his popularity in the presidential election of 1930, where he got over 11 million votes, even though he was eventually defeated by President Hindenburg. But Hitler was helped on the last step to becoming chancellor by right-wing Germans like Von Papen. He persuaded President Hindenburg to appoint Hitler chancellor because he said he would control him. As a result, Hitler was appointed chancellor in January 1933 with three other Nazis in the cabinet.

Hitler now used democracy to destroy democracy. He immediately set about creating a totalitarian dictatorship (which would control all aspects of life – political, social, economic and religious). He called a general election and used terror and propaganda against opponents. He blamed the Reichstag fire on communists. After the election, Hitler passed the Enabling Act, which gave him power to rule by decree. This brought Weimar democracy to an end – all opposition parties were banned, the mass media was controlled and Nazis took over government positions. In the Night of the Long Knives, Hitler eliminated opposition within his own organisation; he used the SS to kill Ernst Rohm and other leaders of the SA who threatened his leadership. When President Hindenburg died, Hitler combined the office of president and chancellor and became Der Führer (The Leader).

Germany's social and economic problems were the main cause of Hitler's rise to power. However, it was the way in which Hitler exploited these conditions that made him successful. Other political parties such as the communists tried to use the same conditions to gain power, but it was Hitler and the Nazis who were successful. He focused on gaining power and used all means to achieve this. Once he became chancellor, Hitler used the power of the state to create a totalitarian dictatorship. In the end, it was as much Hitler's political ability as the circumstances of the time which allowed his rise to power.

Essay: How did Hitler and the Nazis consolidate power and create a totalitarian dictatorship after coming to power in 1933?

Hitler became chancellor of Germany in January 1933. His rise to power had been rapid. In 1928, Hitler and the Nazi Party had only twelve seats in the Reichstag. By 1932, they were the largest party, with 230 seats. Hitler's popularity depended on the weaknesses of the Weimar government, which was blamed for defeat in World War I, accepting the harsh Treaty of Versailles and for its failure to deal with economic problems. These problems were worsened by the Great Depression of 1929, when the withdrawal of American loans led to a rise in German unemployment from 1 million to 6 million. Hitler's policies appealed to the discontent of the industrialists, the middle class and nationalist Germans. Once he became chancellor, Hitler used his position to consolidate his power.

Hitler had been appointed chancellor democratically by President Hindenburg. Now he intended to use democracy to create dictatorship. He called an election for March 1933, hoping to win an overall majority. He enrolled the SA and SS into the police and used legal terror against opponents, especially the communists. When a Dutch communist set fire to the Reichstag, Hitler was able to use the occasion to attack and imprison the opposition and to get emergency powers. Even though he failed to gain an overall majority in the general election, he was able to link up with the Nationalist Party to achieve that majority. He then got the Enabling Act passed, which gave him power to rule by decree and ended Weimar democracy.

But Hitler was faced with a challenge to his leadership within the Nazi organisation. Rohm, the leader of the SA, proposed to combine the SA and the German Army into a People's Army. This would give him great power, which would allow him to challenge Hitler. But Hitler saw the danger. He used Himmler's SS to murder 400 of the leadership of the SA, including Rohm, on the Night of the Long Knives. Through this, he consolidated his power over the Nazi organisation and ensured that the German army would be developed to carry out his policy. When President Hindenburg died soon after, Hitler combined the office of chancellor and president to become *Der Führer* (The Leader). In eighteen months, he had made himself dictator of Germany.

But Hitler was not satisfied with the political power he had. He wanted to create a totalitarian regime which controlled the minds as well as the actions of the German people. He achieved this through propaganda and education. Through Goebbels, his Minister of Propaganda, Hitler controlled the press, radio and cinema. His poster was everywhere, his birthday was celebrated and people saluted each other with 'Heil Hitler'. Hitler also used the Nuremberg Rallies, torchlight parades and the Olympic Games to give an impression of Nazi strength and efficiency. In education, children were taught Nazi racial ideas and loyalty to the Führer. Both boys and girls had to join the Hitler Youth or the League of German Maidens. These were used to indoctrinate the youth into Nazi ideas and to create Hitler's totalitarian state.

The churches did not escape from Hitler's control. However, initially Hitler established friendly relations with the Catholic Church. He agreed the Concordat which gave Catholics full freedom to practise their religion. Very soon, though, Hitler harassed Catholic organisations, especially those dealing with youth. This led to the papal letter, *With Burning Anxiety*, which was smuggled into Germany and read at all Masses. This led to further attacks on the Catholic Church, but Hitler failed to fully control it. He had an easier task with the Protestant churches – he merged them into a Reichskirche. While this created some opposition from individual Protestant clergy, Hitler's control was much greater over them than over the Catholic Church.

Hitler also imposed control over the German economy. He wanted self-sufficiency to prepare Germany for war. He boosted the German economy through rearmament. The growth of heavy industry reduced unemployment rapidly, so that by 1939 there was no unemployment. He also built the autobahn to help the movement of troops. These successes increased his control of the country. But he had less success in creating self-sufficiency in food. He needed his future plans for *lebensraum* in the east to avail of the open spaces for food production. This ultimately led to World War II and his downfall.

Hitler was particularly severe on minorities, especially the Jews. He demanded a pure Aryan Germany, so the Jews were persecuted as outcasts. The Nuremberg Laws deprived them of citizenship and banned marriage with 'pure' Germans. They were also banned from the professions. In the Night of the Crystal Glass, Jewish businesses and synagogues were destroyed. By 1939, 600,000 Jews had been reduced by half, either through death or emigration. Hitler's anti-Semitic policy was used to give him greater control of the country.

But Hitler's totalitarian state could not stop growing. His foreign policy led to expansionism to the east. Inevitably, this caused war, which resulted in Hitler's defeat and death and the end of his totalitarian state.

Essay plan: How important was propaganda in establishing and maintaining Nazi control in Germany?

Intro: Propaganda – define, mass media, Hitler's attitude – tell a big lie, *Mein Kampf*, totalitarian state.

1. Rise to power: Role of propaganda, flags, swastika, salutes, uniform, colour, beginning of Nuremberg Rallies, Goebbels.

2. In power – Goebbels: Minister of Propaganda, newspapers, radio – People's Radio.

3. Cult of personality: Wise leader, slogans, photographs, posters, youth and women.

4. Nuremberg Rallies: Speeches, Nazi organisation, Hitler's role, policies.

5. Riefenstahl: *Triumph of the Will*, *Olympia*, cinema, anti-Semitic, newsreels.

6. Education as propaganda, create Nazis, subjects, boys, girls, youth organisations.

Conclusion: Propaganda in WWII, other factors in establishing and maintaining control – terror, economy, foreign policy, downfall.

Essay plan: Church–state relations in Mussolini's Italy and Hitler's Germany

Intro: Italy – large influence in Italy, centre of Catholic Church, Rome, Pope, people Catholic – few Protestants; **Germany** – most people Christian – Catholic in south and Rhineland – Protestantism founded in Germany – more Protestants than Catholics – Mussolini's Italy and Hitler's Germany = totalitarian regimes – control of all aspects of life – clash with churches inevitable.

1. Italy – improved relations: 1870 – conflict over unification of country – Pope lost land; Mussolini in power after March on Rome – Mussolini anti-clerical but needed better relations with Catholic Church; Catholic Church saw Mussolini as barrier to spread of communism so improved relations – compulsory religious education in primary schools – crucifixes (crosses) in classrooms – Mussolini's Catholic marriage ceremony – fascist campaign of Battle of Births supported by Catholic Church; Pope did not support Catholic Popular Party.

2. Lateran Agreements 1929: Two years of negotiations – Pope recognised Italian state – Italian state recognised papal control of Vatican – £30 million in compensation for loss of Rome 1870 – Catholicism sole religion of state – bishops appointed after consulting Mussolini – salaries paid to bishops and priests – religious instruction in state schools – prestige for Mussolini at home and abroad – greatest political success?

3. Further conflict: Fascist view of education – in controlling youth and in propaganda – Mussolini disbanded Catholic youth and student groups – Pope against – lessened Mussolini's control; Charter of Race (Mussolini's anti-Semitic laws) – opposed by Pope –

not strictly enforced – contributed to declining popularity of Mussolini – Pope supported Italy's neutral stance at beginning of WWII – Catholic Church a separate organisation, could not be controlled by Mussolini – failure of his totalitarian state – contributed to his downfall in WWII.

4. Hitler and Catholic Church: Nazi co-ordination – control of everything – totalitarian state; Hitler brought up a Catholic but later hated Jewish–Christ creed – Christianity weak – in power, praised Christianity – churches thought Hitler would be better at maintaining family values than Weimar; Concordat with Catholic Church (1933) – respect rights of Catholic Church if priests stayed out of politics; Hitler soon broke Concordat – fired Catholic civil servants, undermined Catholic youth organisations, priests on trial for currency smuggling, sexual immorality – Nazis said churchmen were involved in politics – Pope Pius XI – *With Burning Anxiety* – smuggled, read at Masses – criticised Nazi treatment of Catholics, told Catholics to resist; further attacks on Catholics – 400 priests in concentration camps by 1939; Catholic Church celebrated German victories in Poland and France – little criticism of Nazi treatment of Jews; WWII – Catholic Church against Nazi policy of euthanasia – Cardinal Galen's letter read at Masses – condemned execution of mentally ill – euthanasia programme not affected by protests; Hitler controlled the Catholic Church but failed to break it – cautious approach of Pope to condemning extermination of Jews – fear of Nazi persecution.

5. Hitler and Protestant churches: Easier to control – greater number of small churches – Hitler founded Reichskirche (national church) – merged regional churches into one church – supported his views on race and leadership – wanted to get rid of Jewish elements in Christianity – encouraged by German Christian movement – Reich Bishop elected – 'Adolf Hitler is the new messiah' – copy of *Mein Kampf* and sword on altar; opposition to Reichskirche led by Pastor Martin Niemoller – founded Confessional Church – 7,000 pastors supported it but persecuted by Nazis – Niemoller arrested, interned to 1945, Dietrich Bonhoeffer executed – 800 Protestant clergy arrested – Confessional Church put up very little resistance to Nazis – weakened and virtually crushed.

Conclusion: Churches very much weakened in Germany by 1939 – could not cope with power of totalitarian state – Hitler Youth and Nazi control of education would destroy churches in long term, to be replaced by full Nazi worship – Catholic Church still strong in Italy, so less danger there; but churches saved by defeat of Hitler and Mussolini in WWII.

Essay plan: Hitler's foreign policy and the causes of WWII

Intro: Loss in WWI, Treaty of Versailles, harsh conditions, public anger at November Criminals; Hitler's aims – destroy Treaty of Versailles (rearm, conscription, remilitarise) – unite all German-speaking people, Greater Germany – create *lebensraum* (living space) in east, self-sufficiency, raw materials, space, leisure, slave labour.

1. Early success and failure: Cautious approach – consolidating power at home; withdrawal from League of Nations, Disarmament Conference – blamed on France – Four Power Pact with Britain, France and Italy to preserve peace in Europe; ten-year Non-aggression Pact with Poland – broke isolation, first attempt at Anschluss with Austria failed – Mussolini; Saar Plebiscite – success.

2. Destruction of Treaty of Versailles: Power consolidated at home, more aggressive foreign policy; formation of Stresa Front of Britain, France and Italy against German threat; Rearmament – Conscription – Luftwaffe – Anglo–German Naval Agreement (navy to 35 per cent of British, no limit to submarines) – advantage to Germany, Remilitarisation of Rhineland amble (Abyssinian crisis) – France, Britain did not stop him; Siegfried Line.

3. Relations with Mussolini: Abyssinia – League of Nations sanctions, Hitler supported Mussolini; breakdown of Stresa Front, Spanish Civil War – helped Franco, Rome–Berlin Axis agreement on Austria, Anti-Comintern Pact with Italy and Japan against communism, Anschluss with Austria – bigger army, surround Czechoslovakia on three sides.

4. Expansion and reaction: Growth of German armed forces, largest in Europe, Hossbach Memorandum – war plans; Sudetenland (German-speaking, Henlein), Munich Conference – Chamberlain, Daladier, Mussolini – Sudetenland given to Germany (Czech defences and heavy industries), weakness of Policy of Appeasement; – takeover of rest of Czechoslovakia – non-German speaking, change in British policy.

[Policy of Appeasement: Explain; reasons for – experience of WWI, Germany harshly treated in Treaty of Versailles, Hitler a barrier to communism, Britain not ready for war; Chamberlain's policy, Churchill objects, France also in favour – divided society – Left and Right – safe behind Maginot Line; Hitler sees policy as a sign of weakness.]

5. Poland and Nazi–Soviet Pact: Hitler claim to Polish Corridor; Britain and France support Poland, Hitler and Mussolini form Pact of Steel – two armed camps; ten-year Non-aggression Pact with Soviet Union (Nazi–Soviet Pact) – reasons (protect back while he attacks west, lessen danger of two-front war, can attack Poland without Soviet Union joining in); – attack on Poland – surrounded on three sides, protected by Nazi–Soviet Pact and Siegfried Line, Britain and France too far away, strongest army; reaction of Britain and France declare war.

Conclusion: Other factors causing WWII – US isolation; failure/weaknesses of League of Nations (no army, sanctions ineffective, unanimous agreement); policy of appeasement; internal weakness of France; Hitler gambled with expansionism; succeeded until Poland.

Essay plan: The Nazis – Anti-Semitism and the Holocaust

Intro: Hitler's ideas in *Mein Kampf*, and Nazis' Twenty-five Point Programme; got anti-Semitic views in Vienna – tradition of anti-Semitism; Germans were master race (Aryans – *Herrenvolk*) – superior, Jews inferior, evil, subhuman, plotting for world domination, scapegoats for wrongs in German society and defeat in WWI; also linked with 'Jewish–Bolshevik' threat; 600,000 in Germany in 1933 (1 per cent of population).

1. First steps in power: Not immediate persecution – Nazis wanted American loans for economy, also trying to consolidate power in other ways; anti-Jewish propaganda, e.g. films, cartoons, in schools; encouraged boycott of Jewish shops, doctors; random attacks by SA; Jews banned from civil service, universities, newspapers; when Hitler was firmly in power began more serious attack on Jews.

2. Nuremberg Laws 1935: Announced at Nuremberg Rally; systematic persecution of Jews – deprived of citizenship, not protected by law, forbidden to marry pure-blooded Germans, quotas set on Jewish students in universities; not allowed to be judges, doctors, dentists, publishers, editors; laws accepted by German public; Nazis used anti-Semitism to increase their hold on Germany (consolidate their power).

3. Kristallnacht (Night of Crystal Glass): Anti-Semitic campaign lessened during Berlin Olympics (1936); later forced to wear Star of David; Polish Jew killed official in German embassy in Paris; SA burned thousands of Jewish shops and 300 synagogues; encouraged by Goebbels; over 100 Jews killed; 20,000 arrested; taken to concentration camps; Jewish community forced to pay for damage; Jews emigrate, e.g. Einstein, 300,000 in Germany by 1939.

4. WWII: Millions of Jews in Poland (1939) and Soviet Union (1941); SS given job of dealing with the Jews; Special Action Units (Einstatzgruppen) used to massacre Jews in Poland and Soviet Union; Nazis began policy of ghettoisation in Poland – Lodz, Warsaw (largest ghetto), enclosed by walls, ghettoes run by Jewish Councils; Jews rounded up from occupied countries; overcrowded, diseased conditions – thousands died; some Jews used for slave labour in factories; ordinary Germans were Hitler's Willing Executioners (fanatics, sadists, following orders).

5. WWII – Final Solution: Plan to deport Jews to Madagascar dropped; Wannsee Conference 1942, led by Heydrich, head of Reich Security – planning of Final Solution – extermination of Jews; six death camps in Poland, e.g. Auschwitz–Birkenau; Jews brought in by trains from different parts of Europe, gas chambers especially for children and women, slave labour to death; Mengele did medical experiments; 6 million overall killed in war (the Holocaust).

Conclusion: Hitler wasted resources running the camps – food, soldiers, guns; contributed to his defeat; Allied soldiers shocked at opening camps; Nuremberg Trials – Nazi war criminals prosecuted; twelve sentenced to death; others to life imprisonment.

[**Jews in Italy:** No experience of racial persecution in Italy; Mussolini did not believe in ideas of racial superiority; by late 1930s, Mussolini under Hitler's influence (Rome–Berlin Axis, Pact of Steel); anti-Semitic laws – Charter of Race – brought into Italy 1938 – Jews deprived of Italian nationality, banned from state jobs, not allowed to marry non-Jewish Italians; Italians and Pope objected; made Mussolini more unpopular].

Essay plan: Society during WWII, including resistance and collaboration

Intro: German control of Europe; size of armies – total war – all resources mobilised for war; role of governments – increased powers.

1. German home front: Civilians – role in war – food and industry (weapons, etc.); women and children workers – forced labour – 7.5 million; prisoners of war – 2.5 million; food shortages – rationing, black market; bombing raids – day and night – Hamburg, Berlin, etc. – effect on civilians, Dresden 30,000 killed.

2. Conquered lands: e.g. France, exports of food to Germany – Denmark, Holland dairy and poultry to Germany, taxes – to pay for occupying troops; labour supply – compulsory for local projects or sent to Germany – 600,000 from France; repression – shootings, mass deportations – work of Gestapo, SS; reprisals – Lidice – assassination of Heydrich, men killed, women to concentration camps and Oradour-sur-Glane – 642 killed.

3. Jews: Anti-Semitism – 3 million Jews in Poland, 4 million in Eastern Europe, including Soviet Union; ghettoes – Lodz, Warsaw; walled, bad conditions, slave labour; Special Action Groups – Poland, Soviet Union, massacres; Wannsee Conference – Final Solution; concentration and extermination camps, Auschwitz, gas chambers, 6 million total.

4. Britain's home front: Conscription – 2 million; reserved occupations; food shortages – rationing, black market; women workers – single to WRNS (navy), WAAF (air force), farms; home defence – protection from invasion – air raid shelters, gas masks, deaths in Blitz: 22,000, evacuation to countryside; Home Guard (Local Defence Volunteers – Dad's Army); effect on industry – longer hours, 7 million women replace men.

5. Propaganda: Purpose – morale, e.g. Battle of Britain – German plane losses exaggerated; use of press, radio and cinema – controlled by censorship; role of Churchill – cigar-smoking, walking in ruins, speeches; entertainment – cinema and theatre; propaganda in

Germany – role of Goebbels – winning the war – easy, losing the war – more difficult – maintain morale.

6. France in the war: Explain collaboration; defeat by Germany; two governments – Occupied Territory and Vichy France – Laval and Petain; why collaborate with Germans – admired Hitler's success – German New Order, collaborated on Jews, conscripted workers, supplies; people collaborated? To make a living, young women and soldiers, criminal gangs, hatred of Britain; German attitude – exploit France, pay large occupation costs; after war, revenge on collaborators.

7. Resistance in France: How? Collecting intelligence, distributing leaflets, boycotting Germans, sabotage; more organised resistance – Combat and France-Tireur; role of French communists – Soviet Union in war, backbone of resistance; General de Gaulle, leader of Free French, accepted as leader of resistance; role of resistance in war – successful? D-Day? Reprisals by Germans; role of resistance in Germany – student groups, passive resistance plots to kill Hitler (July Plot) – failure.

Conclusion: Overall impact of war on civilians – more civilians died than soldiers, destruction of cities and towns, refugees, morale important for success, also war industries.

Division and Realignment in Europe, 1945–92

Essay: With reference to two or more countries, how successful was the 'Sovietisation' of Eastern Europe between 1945 and 1990?

After the Second World War, Stalin, the leader of the Soviet Union, began the process of Sovietisation in Eastern Europe from Poland to Bulgaria. He wanted to set up Soviet-style governments in these countries under the influence of the Soviet Union. The pattern of setting up Soviet-style governments was much the same in each of these countries. After liberating the country, Stalin imposed a pro-Soviet government. This government included communists who had spent the war in Moscow. He ensured that they got important ministries, such as the Ministry of the Interior, which controlled the police. The communists in government then used their positions to undermine the non-communists and establish the so-called people's democracies.

In Poland, after the war, sixteen of the twenty-five members of the Polish government were communists. This resulted in an intense power struggle between the communists (Polish Workers Party, led by Gomulka) and the more popular Peasants Party and the Socialist Party. The communists used terror tactics against the Peasants Party so that when a new election was held in January 1947, many of their leaders were killed or in prison.

The communists eliminated the Socialist Party when Stalin forced them to join with the communists. Not surprisingly, the communists won 80 per cent of the vote in the 1947 election.

Similarly, in Hungary, communists formed a small part of a national government after the war with other parties. However, their control of the Ministry of the Interior allowed them to terrorise members of the most popular party, the Smallholders Party. The leader of the Smallholders Party was arrested for 'offences against the state'. In the next election the communists won 45 per cent of the vote and shortly after, the socialists merged with them. By 1949 they had established a Soviet-style government.

Other Soviet-style governments also took over in Rumania and Czechoslovakia, Bulgaria and Albania. In a few years after the Second World War, Stalin had created a ring of satellite states that were communist and pro-Soviet. Cominform and Comecon (Council of Mutual Economic Assistance) and, later, the Warsaw Pact were established to control the political, economic and military life of these countries.

Once the communist parties had established complete control in the countries of Eastern Europe, they brought in a Soviet-style economy with central planning: 'There is only one road to socialism, the Soviet road.' This meant government control of industry and collectivisation of agriculture. By 1966, 90 per cent of farming land was collectivised, except in Poland, where only about 15 per cent was collectivised. The governments also nationalised existing industry. This was accompanied by a policy of rapid industrialisation, with an emphasis on heavy industry (steel and machinery), as in Russia, and less emphasis on consumer industries.

One exception to the process of Sovietisation was Yugoslavia. Tito, the Yugoslav leader, took a different approach on the road to communism. There was still government ownership of industry, but the factories were managed differently. In agriculture, private ownership accounted for most of the farming land and the rest were state co-operatives. With its own form of communism, Yugoslavia also followed a different foreign policy.

After Stalin's death in 1953, some of the Eastern European countries sought greater freedom from the harsh conditions of Soviet-style rule. In Poland in 1956, workers rebelled against low wages and harsh working conditions. As Poland was being settled, Hungary rose in October 1956. Hungarian students and workers demanded economic and political freedoms. The Soviet leader, Khrushchev, ordered Soviet troops into Budapest and the Hungarian Uprising was crushed. In Czechoslovakia in 1968, Alexander Dubcek wanted 'socialism with a human face'. But Soviet and Warsaw Pact tanks moved into Czechoslovakia, deposed Dubcek and put down any sign of resistance. Once again, a country which seemed to be drifting away from a Soviet-style one-party system was crushed.

It was mainly developments within the Soviet Union itself – Gorbachev's reforms of *glasnost* and *perestroika* – which brought about the collapse of Soviet-style governments in Eastern Europe and the end of Sovietisation. In 1989, when Gorbachev said he would not use the Soviet army to support communist governments in Eastern Europe, one by one these governments collapsed. In May, Hungary began taking down the barbed wire fence along its border with non-communist Austria. Soon after, Poland held its first free elections since the Second World War, with the election of the first non-communist prime minister in Eastern Europe. Thousands of East Germans marched to the Berlin Wall and began the process of dismantling it. Other countries followed so that by the end of 1989, the Iron Curtain which had divided Europe for forty-five years was torn down. The process of Sovietisation had been a failure.

Essay: How and why did the Cold War develop in Europe between 1945 and 1949?

The Cold War developed after the Second World War. It was a time of hostility and tension between the two superpowers, the USSR (Russia) and its allies (East), and the USA and its allies (West). Europe was divided between support for the two superpowers – Western Europe largely supporting the USA and Eastern Europe willingly or unwillingly supporting the Soviet Union. Events in Europe between 1945 and 1949 were central to heightening the tension between the two sides so that by 1949 the Cold War was fully developed.

Tension and hostility rose between East and West because they had two different sets of beliefs (or ideologies). The East represented the communist system, with its totalitarian dictatorships, while the West represented capitalism and democracy. This tension had existed since the communists came to power in Russia in 1917, but the success of the Soviet Union in the Second World War increased it further. Stalin, the leader of the Soviet Union, feared the USA. He was angered during the Second World War about the slowness of the West opening a second front against Hitler and by the West's refusal to share the secrets of the atomic bomb with him.

Stalin's fear of the West and the impact of the German invasion of Russia in WWII led him to develop a buffer zone in Eastern Europe. By taking over the countries there, he hoped to protect the Soviet Union from invasion from the West. The West looked on this as offensive and feared the spread of communism; Churchill, former British prime minister, said 'an iron curtain' was dividing Europe.

After the war, Stalin proceeded with the rapid 'Sovietisation' of Eastern Europe to create the buffer zone. As the Soviet Union liberated the Eastern European countries from Nazi control, Stalin insisted on pro-Soviet governments being formed. Communists were part of these governments. They used their positions to undermine the non-communists in the governments and to set up Soviet-style governments, called people's democracies. In Poland, for example, the Communist Party led by Gomulka used terror tactics against other political parties. Not surprisingly, the communists won the majority of votes in the 1947 general election. Similarly, in Hungary, the communists used their control of the Ministry of the Interior to terrorise leaders of the more popular political parties. The Communist Party won the general election and established a Soviet-style government. Communists also took over in Czechoslovakia and Yugoslavia, where Tito, who led the resistance during the war, was strong enough to set up his own communist government. The Soviet Union had now created a ring of satellite states in Eastern Europe which expanded its sphere of influence, but frightened the West.

The failure of Britain to continue its support for Greece and Turkey against communism drew the USA more into European politics. President Truman of the US promised aid as part of the Truman Doctrine – the US policy to help 'free peoples' to resist communism. This formed the US policy of containment – to limit the spread of communism. Along with the Truman Doctrine, the US also developed the Marshall Plan (or European Recovery Programme) to give aid to the economies of Western Europe. The Soviet Union prevented Eastern European countries from accepting the aid. Instead, the Soviet Union responded to the Truman Doctrine and the Marshall Plan by setting up Cominform to strengthen control over Eastern Europe, and later Comecon to co-ordinate the economic development of the Soviet Union and its allies. Europe was now divided by Cold War tensions more than ever.

But the incident which heightened tension most of all was the Berlin Blockade and Crisis, 1948–49. After the Second World War, Germany was divided into four zones (US, British, French and Russian) and Berlin was divided into four sectors within the Soviet Russian zone. The US and Britain wanted to revive the West German economy, so they launched a new currency, the Deutschmark. The Soviet Union, on the other hand, wanted to keep Germany weak. Stalin sealed off the borders between East and West Germany and blocked all road, rail and canal routes between West Germany and West Berlin. The US and Britain refused to give in. The Western allies organised a massive airlift to supply 2.5 million people in West Berlin, codenamed Operation Vittles. They used three twenty-mile-wide air corridors to fly into three airports with food, medical supplies, coal and petrol.

After ten months, Stalin lifted the blockade in May 1949 when he realised America and Britain would not give in. This was a huge propaganda victory for the West. It was also a victory for the US policy of containment. However, it resulted in the development of two separate countries, West and East Germany, which remained separate for forty-five years, until the end of the Cold War. This led to further clashes over Berlin in the 1950s and early 1960s. The US also formed the North Atlantic Treaty Organisation (NATO) as a military alliance with Canada and ten Western European countries. This provided a unified military command in the event of a war against the Soviet Union. Six years later, the Soviet Union set up the Warsaw Pact. Now there were two hostile military alliances in Europe.

In four years, from 1945 to 1949, the Allies who had fought and defeated Hitler drifted apart. The suspicion, hostility and tension between both sides were increased by events in post-war Europe. By 1949, there was no turning back and the Cold War dominated foreign affairs for the next forty years.

Essay plan: How successful was the Second Vatican Council in responding to changing patterns of religious observance in Europe?

Intro: Summary of changing patterns, need for reform in Catholic Church.

1. Pope John XXIII: Aggiornamento, Commission, agenda, involvement of bishops, Pope Paul VI, aims.

2. Structure of Church: Role of bishops, collegiality, laity, People of God, Mass, later centralising role of Pope John Paul II.

3. Ecumenism: Christian unity, Pope Paul to Jerusalem, Greek Orthodox, observers.

4. Conflict between conservatives and reformers: Later effects, Lefebvre and Tridentine, fall in vocations, Pope John Paul II – conservative in morals, critical in politics.

5. Church and media: Modern technology, during the Council, later use by Pope John Paul II.

6. Modern issues: Justice and peace, human rights, *Humanae Vitae*, medical problems, divorce.

Conclusion: Other factors influencing changing patterns, effect of VC on these?

The USA and the World, 1945–89

Essay: How effective was the US policy of containment in relation to at least two major crises of the Cold War?

The US developed a policy of containment in reaction to what they regarded as communist aggression in the Cold War. This was a time of tension and hostility between the US and the USSR. This policy stated that communism should be contained wherever it existed and not be allowed to expand. President Truman developed this policy based on George Kennan's Long Telegram and supported by Winston Churchill's speech on the Iron Curtain. Over the next forty years, the US used this policy effectively on a number of occasions, but not always with equal success.

The first test for that policy was the Berlin Blockade. Germany was divided into four zones after the Second World War (US, British, French and Russian) and Berlin was divided into four sectors within the Soviet Russian zone. The Truman Doctrine (US help to countries resisting communism) and the Marshall Plan (economic help for the recovery of Europe) had already heightened tension between the US and the USSR. Consequently, when the US and Britain announced their intention to revive the West German economy and to introduce a new currency, the Deutschmark, Stalin, the Soviet leader, reacted strongly. He imposed a road, rail and canal blockade on West Berlin in order to push the Western Allies out of the city and inflict a defeat on the policy of containment. Truman's response was, 'We are going to stay, period.'

The US and Britain organised a huge airlift to overcome the Soviet blockade of Berlin over the winter of 1948–49. By May 1949, Stalin realised that he would not win, so he lifted the blockade. The policy of containment had proved effective on this occasion. However, it needed to be strengthened, as the Berlin Blockade highlighted weaknesses in the Allies' defences. As a result, the US formed NATO (North Atlantic Treaty Organisation) along with Canada and ten Western European countries. But Berlin continued as a centre of crisis in the 1950s, as 3 million East Germans migrated to the more prosperous West. The new Soviet leader, Khrushchev, insisted on a US withdrawal from Berlin, but President Kennedy stood firm. The Soviets admitted defeat by building the Berlin Wall to stop the flow of emigrants. Instead of Soviet expansion, the policy of containment had forced the Soviets to retreat behind the Berlin Wall.

The US policy of containment faced further tests in Korea and Cuba. In 1950, communist-controlled North Korea invaded US-backed South Korea. President Truman committed US troops to Korea in the name of the United Nations. US and Allied troops, led by MacArthur, pushed back the North Koreans. However, North Korea was supported by communist China, so the war developed into a stalemate. Peace was agreed under two new leaders, Eisenhower in the US and Khrushchev in Russia, along the pre-war border. The policy of containment had worked. Cuba provided an equally serious test for containment. Initially, the US policy failed to support the pro-US government and an internal revolution resulted in a communist government led by Castro. Containment also failed with the disastrous Bay of Pigs invasion. But President Kennedy successfully resisted the Soviet attempt to build missile bases on the island and thereby protected the US mainland from direct Soviet attack.

But containment was much less effective in Vietnam. Presidents Truman, Eisenhower and Kennedy gradually built up US help to the South Vietnamese government to resist attacks from the communist Viet Cong and the North Vietnamese army. These presidents, along with Johnson, followed the domino theory, believing that if South Vietnam fell to communism, other countries nearby would also do so. When Johnson became president, he increased US troop levels dramatically after the Tonkin Incident and the Tonkin Resolution. He believed in a military solution for containing communism. The US used search and destroy missions, aerial bombardment (e.g. Operation Rolling Thunder), chemicals and free-fire zones. But they failed to defeat the guerrilla warfare of the Viet Cong and North Vietnamese, as shown by the Tet Offensive.

But worse was yet to come. Johnson was forced to begin talks in Paris with the North Vietnamese and he called a halt to the bombing of North Vietnam. His successor, Nixon, continued to work to end US involvement because of anti-war opposition at home, the cost of the war and his plan to improve relations with communist China. But Nixon's policy of Vietnamisation – the strengthening of the South Vietnamese army to take a greater part in the war – was only partly successful. He agreed to peace terms in Paris in 1973 which led to US withdrawal from South Vietnam. Two years later, North Vietnam invaded South Vietnam and united North and South under a communist leadership. Soon the neighbouring countries of Laos and Cambodia also had communist governments.

The policy of containment had proved ineffective in Vietnam due to military failure and a growing anti-war movement in the US. In the longer term, however, the policy of containment proved effective. It led to a huge arms race between the US and the USSR which the USSR could not afford. President Gorbachev of the Soviet Union realised that he would have to dismantle the missiles and the Cold War to save the Soviet economy. Ultimately this led to the downfall of communism in the Soviet Union. Not only was the policy of containment effective in most of the crises of the Cold War, its overall effect was to give victory to the US in the Cold War.

Essay: Why did the US become involved in armed conflict in Vietnam and why did it eventually withdraw from that country?

Since the nineteenth century, Indochina (Laos, Cambodia and Vietnam) had been part of the French Empire. After the Second World War, Ho Chi Minh and the Vietminh fought the French to gain independence for Vietnam. Ho Chi Minh was supported by Soviet Russia and after 1949 by communist China. President Truman of the US gave financial support to the French and US involvement in Vietnam gradually increased during the 1950s and early 1960s. This was largely because Vietnam was seen as a Cold War conflict.

By the late 1940s, the Cold War (a period of tension and hostility between the USSR and its allies and the US and its allies) was well established. President Truman, influenced by George Kennan's Long Telegram, followed a policy of containment – that the US would contain communism wherever it was and not allow it to spread. Truman was also prepared to extend the Truman Doctrine to Asia to give help to free peoples fighting the spread of communism. This explains his financial support for the French. But Truman was also influenced by the growth of McCarthyism and anti-communist hysteria in the US – he was accused of losing China to communism. He committed the US to war in Korea and to continued support of the French in Vietnam.

But US involvement increased after the French defeat in Dien Bien Phu and the agreement on the Geneva Accords. This set up separate countries in Laos, Cambodia and North and South Vietnam. North Vietnam was led by Ho Chi Minh and his communist Vietminh, and they attacked the US-supported government of South Vietnam. A new US President, Eisenhower, was forced not only to give financial support to the South Vietnamese government, but also to send in the first US military advisers (1,500 by 1960) to help train the South Vietnamese Army. Eisenhower believed in the domino theory – that if South Vietnam fell to communism, then all the countries in South-East Asia would follow like falling dominoes. Similarly, President Kennedy followed the same policy and had increased the number of US advisers to 16,000 by his death in 1963. His use of Special Forces such as the Green Berets was involving the US more and more in armed conflict in Vietnam.

However, when Johnson became president, he could have withdrawn from Vietnam. But he didn't. Johnson was still influenced by the policy of containment and the domino theory. He also inherited President Kennedy's political advisers, such as Secretary of State Robert McNamara. These believed that US power would provide a military solution to the problem. They looked on Vietnam as a Cold War conflict, with Ho Chi Minh supporting the Viet Cong in the south and in turn being supported by Soviet Russia and communist

China. Johnson also felt that US credibility was at stake – no other country would trust the US if they withdrew now. But Johnson had personal reasons for maintaining US involvement – he did not want to be the first president to lose a war.

Even though Johnson won the 1964 presidential election as the peace candidate against the more aggressive republican, Barry Goldwater, he was soon faced with a stark choice – either withdraw from Vietnam or commit large numbers of troops to the war. He made use of the Gulf of Tonkin Incidents when US ships provoked the North Vietnamese to fire on them as they patrolled close to North Vietnam. Johnson gave a deliberately false account of the incidents to influence US opinion and to help the passage of the Tonkin Resolution. This gave him almost unlimited power to wage war against the North Vietnamese and the Viet Cong. Johnson began Operation Rolling Thunder – the bombing of North Vietnam – and he landed the first US combat troops in Da Nang. By 1968, US forces had increased to over half a million.

However, the US failed to understand the war they were fighting – a nationalist guerrilla war. The US commander, Westmoreland, believed that if he got more soldiers he would win the war. Instead, the US use of search and destroy missions, air bombardments with napalm, defoliants to clear the jungle and free-fire zones turned the peasants of South Vietnam against them. Strategic bombing also failed to destroy the largely agricultural economy of North Vietnam. The US was also supporting an unpopular and corrupt government in South Vietnam who refused to bring in reforms to help the peasants. The US belief that military might would win drew them further into armed conflict, but this in turn contributed to their downfall.

US opinion was turning against the war in Vietnam. TV cameras nightly brought news of the war to television screens. Images of burnt villages, public executions and frightened peasants made Americans question what they were doing in Vietnam. People still believed Johnson when he said the bombing was aimed at military targets, but TV news showed otherwise. An anti-war movement began in US universities in 1965 and slowly gathered momentum as the number of US dead and casualties increased. Johnson's claim that the US was winning the war was undermined by the Tet Offensive of 1968, when Vietminh and Viet Cong attacked the major cities of South Vietnam, including the capital, Saigon. Johnson changed US policy by calling a partial halt to the bombing of North Vietnam and beginning peace talks in Paris. The US had begun the process of withdrawing from Vietnam.

This process was continued by the next president, Nixon. Opposition to the war was growing, the US economy was suffering from budget deficits and inflation, the costs of the war were increasing and the US could not defeat the enemy. Nixon also wanted to improve relations with communist China. However, negotiations in Paris proved difficult and Nixon used communist China to pressurise the North Vietnamese. He also introduced a policy of Vietnamisation to strengthen the South Vietnamese Army to take a greater part in the war. But his secret invasion of Cambodia led to increased opposition to the war at home. It also led to the repeal of the Tonkin Resolution and the passing of the War Powers Act to control the president's use of US troops.

Eventually, peace terms were agreed in Paris in 1973 and the US withdrew from Vietnam. The policy of containment had failed. The US continued to give aid to South Vietnam, but it could not stop the North Vietnamese attack in 1975 which united North and South Vietnam under communist leadership. The US had lost 58,000 soldiers, the economy was weakened, society was divided and the powers of the president were reduced. The US had paid a heavy price for its involvement in Vietnam.

Essay plan: How did domestic factors influence US foreign policy between 1945 and 1968?

Intro: Presidents, role in foreign policy, public opinion, elections, mass media.

1. McCarthyism and Red Scare: Define, McCarthy, downfall of China, strengthened containment, impact, heightened tensions, State Deptartment officials – loss of experts, impact on later US policy on Vietnam, view of world and danger of communism.

2. Anti-war movement during Vietnam War: Reasons for, growth of, impact, Johnson and Tonkin Incident; role of media.

3. Anti-war movement: Tet Offensive, impact on Johnson's actions, negotiations, King, Ali, Mailer against war, why?

4. Nixon and Vietnamisation: Negotiations, bombing Cambodia, Kent State, Paris Peace Accords, who won? North invasion, no help from US, why?

5. Race relations: Cold War, national image, Kennedy and Khrushchev in Vienna, Birmingham and 'Bull' Connor, TV pictures, Vietnam – racial discrimination – more blacks against the war.

6. Military–industrial complex: Iron Triangle, define, heighten anti-communism, Kennedy and missile gap in 1960 presidential election, increased tensions.

Conclusion: Overall influence/importance, other factors, e.g. growth of communism, US economic power – Marshall Plan, development of missiles, success of Vietnamese.

Essay plan: Decline of Cold War certainties, 1969–89

Intro: Policy of containment since post-war – contain spread of communism – led to local wars (Korea, Vietnam), huge build-up of arms, danger of nuclear war, cost to government – government debts, new approach by US – why? – impact of Vietnam War.

1. Nixon and Vietnam: Withdrawal from Vietnam – why? Opposition at home, costs of war, soldiers killed, not able to win, improve relations with China; 'peace with honour' – Vietnamisation – gradual withdrawal of US troops, greater part for South Vietnamese army; half withdrawn by 1971, 40,000 left by September 1972; Nixon Doctrine – US would help countries under internal attack, but not send in US troops.

2. Peace: Slow progress, bomb Cambodia and Ho Chi Minh Trail – mad man strategy, prepared to use atomic bombs; anti-war protests – Kent State – four killed – credibility gap – rebellion in Congress – War Powers Act controlled president's use of troops; peace treaty in Paris 1973 – US withdraw, prisoners of war released, further negotiations to decide about North and South Vietnam; containment had failed, especially as North invaded and took over South in 1975, also communist governments in Laos and Cambodia.

3. Nixon and détente – China: Kissinger – National Security Adviser, Secretary of State; secret channels of negotiation bypassed State Deptartment – shuttle diplomacy – growth of imperial presidency; developed policy of détente – improve relations with Soviet Union and China – ease tensions to cut military spending; visit to China – surprise – Cold War warrior, bad relations since 1949 – increase trade, pressure North Vietnam in peace talks, play off China and USSR, presidential election.

4. Nixon and détente – Soviet Union: Met Brezhnev in Moscow – signed SALT I – limited ICBMs and submarine missiles, peaceful co-existence; differences over Arab-Israeli War 1973 – Nixon put US on nuclear alert, both backed down, truce between Egypt and Syria, and Israel; but Nixon still Cold War warrior over Chile – Allende socialist president – US undermined his rule, led to assassination.

5. Ford and Carter and détente: Ford continued détente, Kissinger as Secretary of State; Ford met Brezhnev; later agreed Helsinki Agreement (1975) – respect borders in Europe, freedom of travel, more trade and cultural links, respect human rights; Carter's policies – moral policy (right and wrong); inexperienced; inconsistent policy – favoured arms reduction but critical of USSR treatment of dissidents (political protestors) – increased tensions also over Egypt (Camp David Agreement); SALT II talks agreed in 1979 – limit on missiles and bombers; but Soviet invasion of Afghanistan – US Congress did not ratify SALT II – Carter banned grain sales to USSR, got US to boycott Olympic Games in Moscow – end of détente.

6. Reagan: Aggressive tone to foreign policy – 'evil empire', US arms build-up – START (arms reduction) talks fail – proposed SDI (Strategic Defence Initiative – Star Wars) – wanted to force Russia to back down in arms race (US stronger economy); still wanted to end Cold War tensions; met Gorbachev twice – good relationship – agreed INF Treaty (Intermediate-range Nuclear Forces) – dismantle missiles in Europe; met again in Moscow; collapse of communist state – end of Cold War.

Conclusion: Containment helped end Cold War – Soviet Union could not keep up spending on arms; Reagan's tough policy worked, also friendship with Gorbachev; US now world's dominant power.

Essay: How successful was civil rights agitation in the US during the period 1945 to 1968?

In 1945, the situation for minority racial groups in the US, such as black Americans, remained much as it had been for the previous seventy years. In the southern states of the US, Jim Crow laws were used to segregate blacks and whites. Blacks were also banned from voting. Discrimination against blacks was led by the white supremacist organisation, the Ku Klux Klan. However, just over twenty years later, by 1968, the conditions for blacks and other minority groups had changed radically and they were largely successful in achieving their civil rights.

By 1945, circumstances for black Americans had changed and these changes were instrumental in leading the successful civil rights campaign. Blacks migrated to the cities and became easier to organise through such organisations as the NAACP (National Association for the Advancement of Colored People). They had a new, more educated leadership, many of whom were Christian ministers. Black soldiers fought in the Second World War for democracy and after the war had higher expectations for their own civil and political rights. The black leadership was able to use the mass media to highlight their conditions. This influenced the views of liberal whites in the northern cities of the US. It also influenced the federal government, which wanted to see the US as the leader of the free world during the Cold War against communism.

The first major success in civil rights agitation occurred in education. The NAACP took test cases to the Supreme Court, where Chief Justice Earl Warren issued many verdicts which opened up education to blacks. The first and most important of these was *Brown v. The Board of Education, Topeka, Kansas*. This stated that state laws which required separate public school education for blacks and whites were unconstitutional. However, this was resisted in the southern states by white citizen councils, state governors and the KKK. In

Central High School, Little Rock, Arkansas, nine black students were prevented from entering the school by National Guardsmen. President Eisenhower had to use federal troops to ensure the safety and education of the students.

However, in spite of the success in desegregating education, the process of achieving racial balance in public schools was slow. Whites still went largely to white schools, and blacks to black schools. The Supreme Court supported bussing of blacks to white schools and vice versa. This caused huge conflict, as whites resisted the enforced bussing. The bussing campaign had limited success, as whites living in the suburbs left the public school system and sent their children to private schools. By 1964, only 2 per cent of blacks attended multi-racial schools in the South, while in the North the majority of black students attended schools where they were in the majority.

Civil rights agitation had more success in desegregating the bus system in the South. Here, black leaders relied on non-violent protest after Rosa Parks was arrested and tried for refusing to give her seat to a white passenger in Montgomery, Alabama. The Montgomery Improvement Association, led by Martin Luther King, organised a year-long black boycott of the bus system. In spite of intimidation by the KKK and local police, the arrest of Martin Luther King and bomb threats, the NAACP was successful when they took the Parks case to the Supreme Court. This ruled that the Montgomery bus regulations were unconstitutional. Non-violent protests were also successful in the lunch counter protests to end whites-only lunch counters. The Freedom Riders were also successful in ensuring that the federal government enforced desegregation of interstate buses.

Voting still presented a problem for blacks in the early 1960s in the southern states. These states used local laws to discriminate against blacks and ensure that only a small proportion of blacks could vote. The NAACP selected Selma as a good location to highlight their case because they expected resistance by the police and the state troopers. The Selma to Montgomery March – led on the last section by Martin Luther King – got huge media coverage. It forced President Johnson to bring in the Voting Rights Act 1965, which banned literacy tests for voter registration.

Pressure from the black community forced the federal government to act to eliminate discrimination. The government was concerned about the image of the US that racial conflict and discrimination gave to the world. Presidents Truman and Eisenhower desegregated the armed forces. Eisenhower also set up a Civil Rights Commission to investigate discrimination against blacks. Kennedy introduced a Civil Rights Bill, which was passed by Johnson in 1964. This outlawed discrimination in public places such as restaurants, theatres and sports stadiums. The government outlawed job discrimination and also followed a policy of affirmative action by ensuring that companies on federal contracts provided jobs for minorities.

Other minority groups followed on the example of the black success. Chicanos (Mexican-Americans) and Native Americans also benefited from these Acts. But they also had other difficulties. Chicanos were used illegally as farm labourers in California and Florida. Their leader, Cesar Chavez, used non-violent protests to get better conditions. Native Americans suffered from bad education and housing, but they had to wait until the 1970s before the Indian Self-Determination Act 1975 was passed which gave them control of their reservations.

Essay plan: How significant was the role of Martin Luther King in the civil rights movement?

Intro: Blacks in post-war America – Jim Crow, discrimination, segregation in South – progress of civil rights movement, success by 1960s, end of Jim Crow, Supreme Court decisions, Civil Rights Act 1964, Voting Rights Act 1965, role of Martin Luther King in bringing this about?

1. Montgomery Bus Boycott: Role in as leader, spokesman, arrest, bombing, church, national figure, techniques of Montgomery used in later campaigns – but role of others – Rosa Parks, E.D. Nixon, other black ministers, black people – important.

2. His style and message: Non-violence, peaceful protest, moral and spiritual crusade, integration, speaker/preacher style – 'I have a dream', Washington march, influence on Civil Rights Act, appealed to liberal whites' conscience, use of media – press and TV.

3. Exploited white hatred: Montgomery Bus Boycott – bombing of King, black churches; 'Bull' Connor and Birmingham – set dogs on marchers, hoses on children, arrested them, highlighted by TV; Selma to Montgomery – police attacks on marchers; embarrassed Northern whites.

4. Organisation: Southern Christian Leadership Conference (SCLC) – umbrella group, unofficial leader of civil rights movement by early 1960s, influence on Kennedy (black vote helped his election) and Johnson, could speak to presidents, consulted by them, King knew importance of federal government in passing laws to gain civil rights.

5. Others used non-violent strategy: Tactics of James Farmer and Congress for Racial Equality (CORE) in 1940s – sit-ins and Freedom Rides; lunch counter protests – in Greensboro, North Carolina, led by students, spread around South; Freedom Riders – organised by CORE, desegregate interstate buses; supported by King.

6. Voter registration campaign: 'Crusade for Citizenship', initial failure, Selma campaign – segregationist police chief, King arrested; Selma to Montgomery March, attacked by police, his role, others led the way, stayed within the law, speeches by King, achieved Voting Rights Act 1965.

7. Other factors: National Association for the Advancement of Colored People (NAACP) strategy of testing cases in Supreme Court – pre-dated King; King marginal role in education, e.g. *Brown v. Board of Education, Topeka, Kansas* – Central High School, Little Rock, Arkansas – Meredith and University of Mississippi.

Conclusion: Break-up of civil rights movement in mid-1960s, challenge to King, Malcolm X, King moved to social and economic problems, anti-Vietnam, Poor People's Campaign, lost white middle-class support, assassination, national hero, overall significance.

The following essay has been developed from the essay plan/notes above.

Essay: How significant was the role of Martin Luther King in the civil rights movement?

After the Second World War, blacks in America were still largely second-class citizens. In the southern states in particular, they faced discrimination and segregation under Jim Crow laws. However, twenty years later, Jim Crow was largely dismantled through Supreme Court decisions and the passage of the Civil Rights Act 1964 and the Voting Rights Act 1965. While the campaign for civil rights pre-dated Martin Luther King, his leadership played a vital role in speeding up the progress of civil rights by focusing the energies of black Americans and playing on the consciences of white leaders.

Martin Luther King came to prominence during the Montgomery Bus Boycott (1955–56). As president of the Montgomery Improvement Association, King provided the leadership which united black people in the city for a year-long successful boycott. Even though he was young (twenty-six years old), he soon became the recognised spokesman for the boycott. His own arrest (twice) and the bombing of his house elevated a local boycott to national news and him to national prominence. The techniques developed in Montgomery were used in later campaigns. However, while King became the recognised leader of the boycott, the success was also due to the work of many others – from Rosa Parks to E.D. Nixon, other black ministers, the commitment of poorer black people of the city and a final decision by the Supreme Court.

It was in Montgomery that King developed his style and message. He advocated non-violence and peaceful protest to achieve his aims. He made the civil rights campaign into a moral and religious crusade. He believed in integration of blacks and whites, not in making adjustments to segregation or separation of blacks and whites. His message became

the dominant message amongst blacks. By the early 1960s, he was clearly the accepted leader of black America, and this was cemented by his 'I Have a Dream' speech at the end of the march in Washington. In turn, the march contributed to the passage of the Civil Rights Act 1964, which outlawed discrimination according to race. King's role was significant in bringing the problems of the South to liberal northern whites through the use of mass media (press and TV).

King deliberately exploited white hatred to achieve a high moral ground. In the Montgomery Bus Boycott, after his house was bombed, he appealed for peace and calm to an angry black crowd. He encouraged peaceful protest in spite of attacks on blacks and the bombing of black churches. Later, in Birmingham, Alabama, he used the racism of police chief 'Bull' Connor to undermine support for segregation. TV pictures showed Connor turning police dogs on marchers and later powerful water cannons on black children. Children were slammed against trees and their clothes were ripped off them. Some were arrested later, as were pregnant women. King deliberately chose children to exploit white hatred and to embarrass northern whites into reacting against segregation. This was important in progressing civil rights.

After the Montgomery Bus Boycott, King founded the Southern Leadership Christian Conference (SCLC) to co-ordinate action for civil rights. This acted as an umbrella group for other civil rights organisations and propelled King to become unofficial leader of the civil rights movement by the early 1960s. He influenced the black vote in the 1960 presidential election which helped elect President Kennedy. He was consulted by Kennedy and his brother, Robert, who was Attorney General, and used government influence in favour of civil rights. King knew that the federal government was central in achieving civil rights for blacks. He appealed to the American Constitution and to American democracy and used Cold War rivalry to highlight the treatment of blacks. This forced the federal government through Johnson to pass the Civil Rights Act and the Voting Rights Act and to use affirmative action, which forced quotas of black workers on companies winning federal contracts.

But King wasn't the only source for this non-violent, direct action strategy. In the 1940s, James Farmer and the Congress for Racial Equality (CORE) used sit-ins and Freedom Rides to highlight racial segregation, but without success. In the 1960s, university students began the lunch counter protests with sit-ins in a segregated restaurant in Greensboro, North Carolina. This led to widespread use of sit-in protests in many areas of segregated life in the southern states. CORE used Freedom Rides on interstate buses to force the federal government to enforce desegregation. Both methods had significant success – 50,000 students were involved in the sit-ins – and they forced the federal government to intervene to support desegregation. In these cases, Martin Luther King could only provide moral support for the work of students and CORE.

In the voter registration campaign, King also faced failure before he achieved success. His 'Crusade for Citizenship' – to encourage blacks to register to vote – failed initially. When it was tried in Selma, it was helped by the actions of a segregationist police chief. He arrested King, which gave national coverage to the Selma campaign for voter registration. When a march from Selma to Montgomery was organised to highlight their cause, it was attacked by police. King ensured that blacks did not respond with violence. He also began the renewed march, which eventually reached Montgomery in a blaze of publicity. The success of King in providing leadership for the Selma march forced President Johnson to sign the Voting Rights Act to end voter discrimination against blacks.

But King played little role in desegregating education. Instead, much of the initiative for this came from the policy of the NAACP (National Association for the Advancement of Colored People) of testing cases in court. This led to the *Brown v. The Board of Education, Topeka, Kansas* case which ruled that segregated schooling was unconstitutional. Neither was King involved in Central High School, Little Rock, Arkansas when nine young black students eventually gained admittance to the school with the help of federal troops. It took the case of James Meredith, who enrolled in the University of Mississippi, to break segregated education there. The success in desegregating education was therefore due to others, not King.

By the mid-1960s, the civil rights movement had achieved many of its goals. It was also in the process of breaking up, as King's leadership and methods were challenged by other leaders such as Malcolm X. King's efforts to broaden civil rights to social and economic equality by working for poorer blacks in the northern cities failed. His anti-Vietnam stance undermined his influence with Johnson's federal government. His Poor People's Campaign lost white middle-class support. When King was in the process of organising the Poor People's March on Washington, he was assassinated by a white racist. His tragic death elevated him to the status of a national hero and it enlarged his role in the civil rights movement. While he played a vital role in providing practical and moral leadership for black Americans, he was just one factor in accounting for the success of the civil rights movement.

Essay plan: To what extent can the moon landing (1969) be seen as both a major advance in technology and as a statement of American foreign policy?

Intro: Kennedy's commitment, *Apollo 11* on moon, factors which influenced it – Cold War, technology, also economic power.

1. Influence of US foreign policy: What was the Cold War, success of Soviet space exploration – *Sputnik*, Gagarin, national security, capitalism vs. communism, NASA founded, context for Kennedy's speech.

2. Advances in rockets/missiles: Nuclear war, ICBM – *Atlas*, *Titan* rockets, Cold War rivalry, role of military–industrial complex.

3. Space technology: Challenge to US technology, projects to overcome obstacles to moon landing, Mercury Project – Shepard, Glenn – three orbits.

4. Gemini projects: Two-man space flights, rendezvous and docking, space walks, *Surveyor* space flights – testing and photographing surface of moon, *Lunar Orbiter* – photo sites.

5. Apollo mission: Testing Saturn rocket, three-man spacecraft, setback with *Apollo 7* – three die, *Apollo 8* – orbit of moon and return, TV, *Apollo 9* – docking, *10* – lunar module tested.

6. Moon landing: *Apollo 11*, three modules, most powerful rocket, three astronauts, simulators, weightlessness, spacesuits, freeze-dried food, scientific experiments, heat shield, computers.

Conclusion: *Apollo 11*, huge project – 400,000 employees, $25 billion, US ahead of Soviet technology, later landings, space stations and shuttle, later Star Wars.

Essay plan: How successful was Harry Truman as president of the United States?

Intro: Vice-president, attitude to presidency, buck stops here, seven years as president.

1. A-bomb: Reasons for dropping, Stalin, Potsdam, end of war, success?

2. Containment: Attitude to communism, define, reasons for, US foreign policy for next forty years, also policy of deterrence, success?

3. Truman Doctrine, Marshal Plan: Explain, effects, success?

4. Berlin Blockade: Reasons, Truman's attitude – test for containment, quote: 'We are going to stay, period', success? NATO.

5. Korean War: Containment, US involvement – police action, Truman and McArthur, success?

6. 1948 presidential election: Face to face, whistle-stop, ordinary people, unexpected success, also Congress victory, defended Roosevelt's New Deal.

7. Domestic policy: Twenty-one-point programme, bad relations with Congress, Fair Deal – social security, housing, civil rights, executive orders and racial segregation in armed forces, civil service, GI Bill of Rights.

Conclusion: Overall view – better record in foreign policy, policy followed by others – led to Vietnam, but also downfall of communism, attitude to McCarthyism, but highlighted communism, National Security Act – set up CIA, Loyalty Boards, growing reputation among historians.

Essay plan: With particular reference to at least two presidencies, to what extent did the power and role of the US president change between 1945 and 1973?

Intro: Role of president, six main functions – brief explanation, separation of powers.

1. Factors in growth of power: Crises, more complicated society, more active government, unifying force, imperial presidency.

2. Roosevelt's role: Mostly pre-1945, so be very careful, maybe use as part of another paragraph, e.g. brief mention of New Deal and WWII expanding power.

3. Truman: Foreign policy, buck stops here, Korean War, executive orders, limits to his power by Congress.

4. Kennedy: Power of Congress, e.g. Civil Rights Bill, Kennedy's relationship with, Kennedy's interest in foreign policy, Cuban Missile Crisis.

5. Johnson: Attitude to role of federal government, Johnson Treatment, negotiation with Congress, use of Kennedy's death, Great Society, Civil Rights.

6. Johnson: Vietnam War, Tonkin Resolution, Tet Offensive, anti-war movement, mass media – set limits.

7. Nixon: Personality, Supreme Court judges, role of FBI, CIA, Watergate, bombing of Cambodia, anti-war movement, Congress – new laws to limit president, declining prestige.

Conclusion: Power and role, growth of civil service, presidential bureaucracy, decline in prestige during Ford and Carter but restored by Reagan.

Essay plan: Johnson – the presidency, Vietnam, Great Society

Intro: Texan, poverty in youth, teacher, sympathy for poor, FDR his hero; long political experience – senator, vice-president, believed in power of government to improve lives of people; assassination of JFK, sworn in as president, won presidential election 1964, democratic majority in Congress, strove to be great.

1. Great Society – war on poverty: Michael Harrington, *The Other America* – 25 per cent

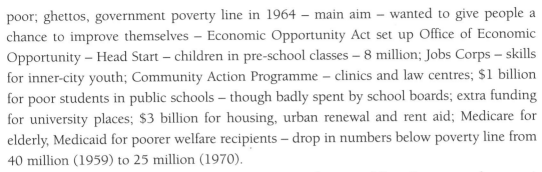
poor; ghettos, government poverty line in 1964 – main aim – wanted to give people a chance to improve themselves – Economic Opportunity Act set up Office of Economic Opportunity – Head Start – children in pre-school classes – 8 million; Jobs Corps – skills for inner-city youth; Community Action Programme – clinics and law centres; $1 billion for poor students in public schools – though badly spent by school boards; extra funding for university places; $3 billion for housing, urban renewal and rent aid; Medicare for elderly, Medicaid for poorer welfare recipients – drop in numbers below poverty line from 40 million (1959) to 25 million (1970).

2. Economy: Grew under LBJ – GNP grew, unemployment fell to 5 per cent due to tax cuts, world economic growth and military spending; but growing budget deficit (Keynesian influence) – to pay for Great Society and Vietnam War; greater spending than income from taxes; small deficit – Johnson government borrowed – more money – inflation began from 1965 onwards – main economic problems began after his presidency but partly due to his policies.

3. Civil rights: Most significant role of any president; Kennedy brought in Civil Rights Bill but failed to pass it; Johnson used power of persuasion with Congress (Senate and House of Representatives) to pass Civil Rights Act 1964 – outlawed discrimination on basis of race, sex, religion; impact of Selma march on him; Voting Rights Act 1965 – federal role in voter registration – no literacy and other tests for voters; affirmative action – companies on federal contracts had quotas of black workers; crucial role in eliminating legal basis for racism.

4. Vietnam War: Reasons for – domino theory, US credibility, military solution, not first president to lose a war; inherited war – withdraw or greater commitment? – knew little about foreign policy, kept on Kennedy's advisers – Tonkin Incident used as excuse for greater commitment – Tonkin Resolution – allowed to take 'all necessary steps' – increased numbers of soldiers to half a million by end of 1967; large-scale bombing (Operation Rolling Thunder), $30 billion a year by 1968; but growth of anti-war – divisions in US; Tet Offensive – withdrawal from presidential race, began withdrawal from Vietnam (reasons: cost, deaths) – impact of Vietnam War on presidency – distraction from Great Society – 'that bitch of a war'.

5. Presidency: Extended federal power – worked hard – centralised control in White House; power over Congress – Johnson Treatment – 3B Congress: bullied, badgered, brainwashed – use of sympathy after death of President Kennedy – Civil Rights Act, Voting Rights Act; new poverty programmes – federal agencies – huge number of federal laws, especially in first two years – passed more reform laws in eighteen months than other presidents in two terms (i.e. eight years); Tonkin Resolution increased power – deceived public on involvement in Vietnam – did not provide full information – while his style and methods worked for domestic policy, they failed for foreign policy because he did not want to listen to the advice of others.

Conclusion: Tragic presidency – on the verge of greatness, but spoiled by failure of Vietnam War; genuine concern for poor and blacks, political skills to achieve aims – but poor speaker, afraid of media, failed to bring people along – however, created a 'more caring and just nation' – greater interest and knowledge of domestic affairs – main aim = Great Society but distracted by 'that bitch of a war' – only American president to lose a war; but also improved environment – slum clearance, forty-five national parks, protected species of animals and trees, cleaning up rivers – ahead of his time?

Essay plan: What problems were caused by youth culture, counterculture and multiculturalism in the US between 1950 and 1989?

Intro: Consensus in US in post-war (1945 to early 1950s) – optimism, melting pot working, patriotism, religion stronger, Cold War – anti-communist, American dream; collapsed in 1960s, America divided by late 1960s.

1. Youth culture: Baby boom after WWII; during 1950s more students attended high school, colleges, universities; benefited from affluent society; teenagers became a target for business – advertising, TV; spent more on themselves than the national income of smaller European countries; youth culture led to generation gap with adults; wanted more freedom – do things their own way; J.D. Salinger's *The Catcher in the Rye;* rock 'n' roll, Elvis Presley, Chuck Berry, The Twist; the Beatles in the 1960s; hairstyle and clothes.

2. Delinquents and sexual revolution: Adults alarmed at rise of delinquents (young people in trouble with police) – increase in number of fights and teenage drinking parties; US Senate investigated problem; some blamed violent comics – states passed regulations to control publication; others blamed movies, e.g. *Rebel without a Cause* (James Dean); sexual revolution in 1960s – invention of the Pill in 1961 led to increase in casual sex, spread of venereal diseases; in 1980s, virginity and celibacy become more popular.

3. Counterculture, hippies, anti-war movement: Rejected prevailing consumer culture, mainly middle-class white, dropped out of university; colourful clothes, beads, long hair, communal living, free love, marijuana; flower people, anti-war – spoke of peace, love and beauty; linked to wider anti-war movement begun in universities (Students for a Democratic Society) – (Vietnam = civil war, brutality of war, keep money for Great Society) – later spread after Tet Offensive to wider society, also senior politicians Eugene McCarthy, Robert Kennedy – divided US society.

4. Mistrust of government: After Vietnam War, great division in American society; Pentagon Papers leaked to *New York Times* and *Washington Post*; showed government had deceived public over war; secret bombings of Cambodia under Nixon – led to credibility gap, deaths in Kent State protest; Watergate crisis – break-in at Democratic Party headquarters led to further mistrust; attempt at cover-up; image of presidency and government suffered greatly.

5. Multicultural and ethnic pride: America became melting pot with immigrants from all over the world settling there; expected to follow the American Way; growth of ethnic pride challenged this idea; civil rights movement made people more aware of their roots; black leaders encouraged pride in their history; Chicanos demand education in Spanish; Native Americans pursued a cultural revival; led to clash of opinions on multiculturalism – some believed it provided greater tolerance and inclusiveness in society; others believed it undermined a united country, dumbing down in education.

6. Urban poverty: Blacks migrated from South to northern cities for work; whites moved to suburbs – loss of tax revenue to cities, city centres became black ghettoes – high unemployment, poor education; bad social and economic conditions led to urban riots – begun in Watts district, Los Angeles, spread to Chicago, San Francisco and Detroit; rioters argued that there were barriers to improvement; radical leaders such as Malcolm X advocated violence; drugs widespread in ghettoes, criminals mostly young, black and male – tension between black youths and police often sparked off incidents.

Conclusion: Government policies were affected – crime became a major election issue; successive presidents concentrated on job training, education and better housing – Johnson brought in Medicaid and Medicare; Reagan cut back on welfare with his Reaganomics policy – destroyed progress made by previous presidents in relation to social problems in America.

Essay plan: Why was there an economic boom in the United States between 1945 and 1968?

Intro: Boom from end of Second World War to 1968; economy doubled, unemployment low, inflation low (2.5 per cent), US greatest economic power.

1. Impact of Second World War: War industries, eliminate unemployment, women in workforce, growth of savings, consumer boom, greater government revenue, more taxes, larger company profits – investment in technology, US exports to war damaged Europe, Marshall Plan.

2. Increased government spending (public investment): 600 times from 1940 to 1980, influence of Keynesian ideas, defence spending due to Cold War – conscript army, two wars – Korea and Vietnam, weapons research and development – missiles, airplanes, etc., growth of military–industrial complex – space exploration, man on moon, $25 billion.

3. Increased government spending: GI Bill of Rights, aid to veterans, houses, business, education, 8 million by 1956, Highways Act 1954 – roads, construction, interstate trade, cars, trucks, cheaper oil, roadside restaurants, tourism; social welfare, New Deal and Great Society of 1960s, welfare benefits to reduce poverty, job training programmes, greater skills.

4. Technological advances, increased investment, more at university, increased productivity (output per worker), better wages for workers, more spending, e.g. invention of transistors – used in development of weapons, computers, household appliances, electronics industry, computer industry – 1 million employed 1990, $150 billion output.

5. Development of multinational corporations, mergers, could invest in research and development, invested abroad to create world market, greater globalisation – spread of American products e.g. Coca-Cola, IBM.

6. Growth of population: 95 million between 1940 and 1980, increased workforce and market for goods, changed age structure – more younger people, part of growing teen market, part of larger consumer society spurred on by affluence, low interest rates, credit cards, advertising.

Conclusion: Impact of boom; consumer society – cause and consequence of economic boom; increased sales of cars; food outlets – more eating out, household appliances – more women in the workforce, spread of TV and leisure; greater divisions in society between rich and poor – provoked racial riots in late 1960s.